Christmas

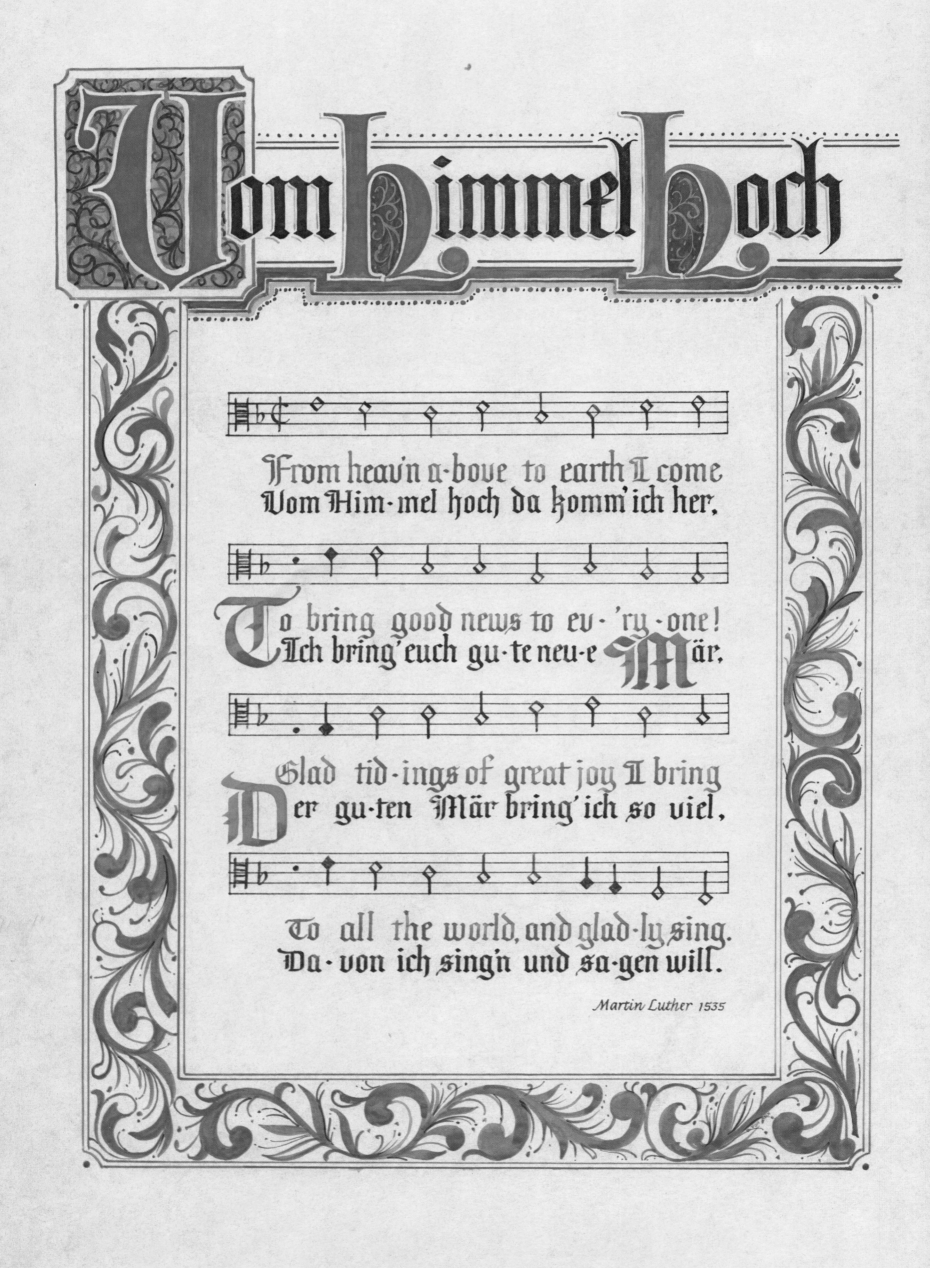

Christmas

The Annual of Christmas Literature and Art

FOUNDED BY RANDOLPH E. HAUGAN, EDITOR VOLUMES ONE THROUGH FIFTY

Volume Fifty-three

Augsburg Publishing House
Minneapolis, Minnesota

Christmas Gospel   5

Christmas Classic   24

Christmas Nostalgia   26

Christmas Music   33

Christmas Customs   40

Table of Contents

Editorial staff: Leonard Flachman, Karen Walhof, Jennifer Fast; Allan Mahnke, music.

Copyright © 1983 Augsburg Publishing House.
All rights reserved. Manufactured in the United States of America.
Library of Congress Catalog Card No. 32-30914
International Standard Book No. 0-8066-8962-5 (paper) 0-8066-8963-3 (cloth)

The Christmas Story

According to St. Luke and St. Matthew

And it came to pass in those days that a decree went out from Caesar Augustus that all the world should be registered.

This census first took place while Quirinius was governing Syria.

And all went to be registered, everyone to his own city.

And Joseph also went up from Galilee, out of the city of Nazareth, into Judea, to the city of David, which is called Bethlehem, because he was of the house and lineage of David, to be registered with Mary, his betrothed wife, who was with child.

And so it was, that while they were there, the days were completed that she should be delivered.

And she brought forth her firstborn son, and wrapped him in swaddling cloths, and laid him in a manger; because there was no room for them in the inn.

And there were in the same country shepherds living out in the fields, keeping watch over their flock by night.

And behold, an angel of the Lord stood before them, and the glory of the Lord shone around them, and they were greatly afraid.

The Madonna in the Landscape (1511-1512) by Matthias Grünewald. This painting is one of nine panels Grünewald (Matthis Gothart Neithart) painted for a folding altarpiece originally in the Antonite abbey chapel at Isenheim, France. It extols the glorification of Jesus and Mary made possible by his birth. The monumental foreground figure of Mary, which creates a pyramidal foil for the Christ child, shows Italian Renaissance influence. Her sumptuous red gown displays Grünewald's interest in the effects of iridescent color and light. The two golden rosary beads Jesus holds symbolize Mary's glorification, while his tattered swaddling cloths, hints of his future suffering, symbolize Christ's glorification. (He wears a similar tattered loincloth on the crucifixion panel of this altarpiece.) The closed garden, its fig tree, and red roses allude to Mary's virgin motherhood. Details in the landscape are similar to those in two of Dürer's engravings. Its Eden-like setting proclaims that paradise is regained through Jesus' birth. The unidentified abbey and da Vinci-like mountains allude to Mount Zion. An annunciation to the shepherds with colossal ghostly figures and God with the angelic host complete this ethereal vision. Grünewald, a peripatetic figure for whom painting was but one of many vocations, captured the mystical faith of his age in this painting. (See page 5.)

The Annunciation to the Shepherds (c. 1480) by Hans Memling. This detail from a long narrow panel of scenes depicting the lives of Christ and the Virgin Mary was painted by Memling for a member of the Bruges tanners' guild. Its daytime setting lacks the drama of a nighttime version, as in Cranach's distant scene. The angel's message is given and received very calmly, except for the dog, whose head is raised to bark or howl. Memling's treatment of this contrived section of landscape with its buildings and figures indicates his interest in perspective. He set up numerous diagonals in the placement of the figures, the vegetation, the roof lines, and even the bagpipes and staffs to convey a sense of depth and space. The angel and standing shepherd balance each other, as do the two seated shepherds, while the circle of sheep and the dog give further order and unity. The figures of the angel and shepherds are delicate and slender, while the colors of their clothing complement those in the landscape and add to its serenity. It appears that the angel has just interrupted their music-making, another example of Memling's charming treatment. The balance, depth, and unity of this scene is characteristic of his mature style. Memling's concern for artistic problems and clarity of style made him the leading guild painter of Bruges during the last half of the 15th century.

And the angel said to them, "Do not be afraid, for behold, I bring you good tidings of great joy which will be to all people.

"For there is born to you this day in the city of David a Savior, who is Christ the Lord.

"And this will be a sign to you: You will find a babe wrapped in swaddling cloths, lying in a manger."

And suddenly there was with the angel a multitude of the heavenly host praising God and saying: "Glory to God in the highest, And on earth peace, good will toward men!"

And so it was, when the angels had gone away from them into heaven, that the shepherds said to one another, "Let us now go to Bethlehem and see this thing that has come to pass, which the Lord has made known to us."

And they came with haste and found Mary and Joseph, and the babe lying in a manger.

And when they had seen it, they made widely known the saying which was told them concerning this child.

And all those who heard it marveled at those things which were told them by the shepherds.

But Mary kept all these things and pondered them in her heart.

And the shepherds returned, glorifying God for all the things that they had heard and seen, as it was told to them.

The Nativity of Christ (c. 1520) by Lucas Cranach the Elder. Cranach's night nativity captures the awe and mystery of the Christ child's birth. Joseph, Mary, and the oxen form a large and protective triangle around the child. Rays of light illuminate all the surrounding figures, overpowering the light from the candle Joseph holds. The rays remind us of the words from John's gospel about the true light who came into the world. This contrast between divine and human light recalls a description of the nativity by St. Birgitta that influenced versions by some 15th century painters. Those adoring cherubs, who surround the infant like a celestial bodyguard, are similar to Italian cherubs *(putti)*. The elderly Joseph contrasts with a youthful Mary, who kneels in rapt adoration. This has been her posture in nativity scenes since the late Middle Ages. Partially illumined by the child's divine light, the wondering shepherds are reminders of his humble humanity. The velvety darkness provides a dramatic foil for the holy family and their visitors, while hiding their surroundings. At the same time, the annunciation to the shepherds takes place in the distance, a device used by some late medieval artists. In his refined and touching rendition of the nativity, Cranach used rich colors and light to make his soft figures merge with the darkness as they adore the "true light" in their midst.

Now after Jesus was born in Bethlehem of Judea in the days of Herod the king, behold, wise men from the East came to Jerusalem, saying, "Where is he who has been born King of the Jews? For we have seen his star in the East and have come to worship him."

When Herod the king had heard these things, he was troubled, and all Jerusalem with him.

And when he had gathered all the chief priests and scribes of the people together, he inquired of them where the Christ was to be born.

And they said to him, "In Bethlehem of Judea, for thus it is written by the prophet:

'And you, Bethlehem, in the land of Judah, Are not the least among the rulers of Judah; For out of you will come a Ruler, Who will shepherd my people Israel.'"

Then Herod, when he had secretly called the wise men, determined from them what time the star appeared.

And he sent them to Bethlehem and said, "Go and search diligently for the young child, and when you have found him, bring back word to me, that I may come and worship him also."

When they had heard the king, they departed; and behold, the star which they had seen in the East went before them, till it came and stood over where the young child was.

When they saw the star, they rejoiced with exceeding great joy.

And when they had come into the house, they saw the young child with Mary his mother, and fell down and worshipped him. And when they had opened their treasures, they presented gifts to him: gold, frankincense, and myrrh.

And being warned by God in a dream that they should not return to Herod, they departed for their own country another way.

Adoration of the Magi (1504) by Albrecht Dürer. Dürer painted this panel to adorn the castle church at Wittenberg of Elector Frederick the Wise. Influences from the Italian Renaissance are present. The imposing figures occupy a stagelike setting close to the picture plane. Their elegant, idealized forms compose a pyramid, accented by the stable's roof lines and the nearby masonry. The arches and rearing horse in the distance reveal Dürer was familiar with Leonardo da Vinci's noted unfinished painting of the Magi's visit. Italian influences are evident as well in his treatment of the landscape, lighting, perspective, and scale. The ruined building alludes to the Old Testament messianic prophecies now fulfilled in Christ. An exotic note was added to the iconography by including the black Moorish king, a subject other northern Renaissance painters from the 16th century, such as Bosch and Bruegel, repeated in their versions of the Magi's visit. Dürer painted himself here, posing as the richly dressed magus standing behind Mary and the infant Jesus. The elegant and richly colored clothing of the Magi and the virgin makes them stand out against the muted background. As another personal touch, Dürer added the date of this painting and his monogram to the stone slab on Mary's right. This is one of the most important works of Dürer, who is remembered both for his paintings and his engravings.

The Rest on the Flight to Egypt (c. 1510) by Gerard David. Flemish and Italian approaches are combined in David's small panel. The monumental foreground figure of Mary is done in the Italian Renaissance manner, a reflection of its increasing influence upon northern painters after 1500. But she is placed in a landscape whose detailed naturalism and disguised symbolism reflect the traditions of 15th century Flemish painting. Her rocky seat stands for Christ, while the grapes she offers him point to his Last Supper and passion. The plants in the foreground signify virtues associated with Mary and her Son: the fern and violet, humility; the cyclamen, Mary's sorrows; the strawberry plant, righteous-

ness. A beautifully executed wicker basket shows the meticulous attention David gave to details. As the ass stands patiently by, Joseph flails a chestnut tree (a symbol of chastity) for some nuts. David related this biblical episode to the daily life of his era by garbing the holy family in the clothing worn then and by placing them in a Flemish rather than in an Egyptian landscape. The holy family's calm and sober manner is complemented by the landscape's peaceful and spacious atmosphere and by the use of rich, restrained colors. The graceful serenity of this imagined informal moment shows why David became the leading painter of Bruges after 1494.

And when they had departed, behold, an angel of the Lord appeared to Joseph in a dream, saying, "Arise, take the young child and his mother, flee to Egypt, and stay there until I bring you word; for Herod will seek the young child to destroy him."

When he arose, he took the young child and his mother by night and departed into Egypt, and was there until the death of Herod, that it might be fulfilled which was spoken by the Lord through the prophet, saying, "Out of Egypt I have called my son."

But when Herod was dead, behold, an angel of the Lord appeared in a dream to Joseph in Egypt, saying, "Arise, take the young child and his mother, and go into the land of Israel, for those who sought the young child's life are dead."

And he arose, took the young child and his mother, and came into the land of Israel.

The Artists. These five painters were all northern Europeans active during Martin Luther's lifetime. Memling and his pupil David were Flemish (from what is now Belgium), while Grünewald, Dürer, and Cranach were German. Painting on wooden panels, they developed very different styles; all but Memling were influenced by Italian art. The figures in each of the pictures shown portray the reserve and solemnity that was characteristic of northern painting from that era. Disguised symbolism was employed by all five artists, though Grünewald's and David's paintings surely present more complexity and effectiveness in its use. Influences from the Italian Renaissance are evident in the works of Grünewald, Cranach, David, and especially Dürer. Each one placed his subjects in a landscape, which was treated very differently. Grünewald's landscape is ethereal and mystical; Memling's is simplified and stylized; Cranach's is nocturnal; Dürer's is idealized; and David's is detailed and naturalistic. Born within five years of each other, Grünewald, Dürer, and Cranach were sympathetic to Martin Luther and to his reforming efforts; moreover, Cranach was Luther's personal friend and painter. We are privileged to be among the many generations who can enjoy the magnificent and priceless visual legacy these five artists left behind. Our Christmas celebration is enriched by their vision.

Luther's Influence on the Customs of Christmas

LA VERN J. RIPPLEY

During 1983 communities around the world have commemorated the 500th anniversary of the birth of Martin Luther, the great reformer, on November 10, 1483. In Germany the cities of Berlin, Darmstadt, Hamburg, Heidelberg, Mainz, Nürnberg, Stuttgart, Tübingen Wolfenbüttel, and Worms among others staged special functions to mark the occasion. In most cases the focus was not only on the person and the works of Martin Luther, but also on the Reformation as the central fact of recent German history.

Luther's influence was felt not only in the theology of the church, but also in the Christmas traditions. It was customary during the time when the famous churchman lived to celebrate Christmas not just on December 25 but from mid-November to at least Candlemas on February 2. During more than 30 years Luther preached sermons, wrote letters, composed hymns, and devised pageants for children, all of which provide insights into his sense of how Christmas should be celebrated.

Popular legend maintains that Luther was the first person to cut down an evergreen tree, bring it home, and decorate it with candles to "imitate the starry skies of Bethlehem that holy night." Under it, Luther positioned a carved wooden crèche including the figures of Mary, Joseph, and the Child along with various animals. The first Christmas tree of record, however, was one cut in 1604 and displayed in Strassburg, a city on the upper Rhine between Germany and France. The Christmas tree tradition developed rapidly and came to the United States with the Hessian soldiers who fought as mercenaries for the British during the American Revolution. The practice remained unknown in France and other European countries until the mid-19th century. In 1844 it arrived in England when Prince Albert of Saxony and Queen Victoria put up the first English Christmas tree in Windsor Castle. In the United States the tradition continued among the German settlers, but it did not gain national status until 1856 when President Franklin Pierce first decorated a tree in the White House.

Whether Luther deserves the credit for decorating the first evergreen at Christmastime or not, the tradition of erecting a tree at Christmas is quite ancient. Christian churches in the early centuries often hung a tree with fruit, especially apples, on Christmas Eve to commemorate the story of Adam and Eve. By eating the forbidden fruit our first parents made necessary the birth of Christ to redeem humankind.

In like manner, Luther is credited with creating the tradition of cradle singing. Although Luther did write simple songs for children to sing while they rocked the cradle during Christmas Eve services, the cradle-rocking tradition is much older than Luther. Similarly Luther fostered but did not invent the crèche. These visual aids began at least as early as St. Francis of Assisi (d. 1226), who enjoys credit for the idea even though it is probably much older than Francis.

Luther's most timeless contribution to the Christmas season is his hymn, *"Vom Himmel hoch da komm ich her"* ("From heaven above to earth I come"). First printed in the *Klugsche Hymnal* in 1535, the lyrics rest on Luther's oft-repeated saying, "If we want to train children, we have to become children with them." Folk hero that he was, Luther wrote the 16 verses in simple childlike sentences that tell the story of the infant Jesus. Rather than create a new melody, the great hymnist set the words to a simple, well-known folk tune. In the tradition of a folk ballad, the hymn opens when the angel announces:

> From heaven above to earth I come
> To bear good news to every home.
> Glad tidings of great joy I bring
> Whereof I now will say and sing.

Not written by Luther but often credited to him is the carol, "Away in a manger." Of much more recent origin, this cradle song was written to mark the 400th anniversary of Luther's birth in 1885, not in Germany or even in the German language. This world-famous carol was composed in Pennsylvania and first sung in English long before its translation into German. Luther did write other Christmas hymns such as *"Vom Himmel kam der Engel Schar"* with its line, *"Sie sagten ihn'n: ein Kindlein zart, das liegt dort in der Krippe"* ("Behold the tender babe, they said, in yonder lowly manger laid"), which inspired the writer of "Away in a manger." James R. Murray in 1887 innocently ascribed the text to Luther.

Like others contemplating the events of Christmas, Luther often viewed the sacred through the eyes of Germanic folklore. For instance he allowed that there might have been more than three Wise Men present when Christ revealed himself to the Gentiles. The number three, after all, derives from the dominant characteristic in Germanic folklore to report things in units of three. Luther suggested alternatives that preserved this rule: There might have been six (twice three) or perhaps a dozen (three times four) Wise Men.

The first day of the Christmas period for Luther was

not the First Sunday of Advent but the Feast of St. Andreas, November 30. On the night of November 30, according to the ancient tradition, young women learned the identity of their future husbands. In unpublished manuscripts held in Nürnberg, Luther mentions that a sister of his wife, Katherine von Bora, practiced the custom. In his table talks Luther discusses the role of St. Andreas as a "coupler" and as the patron saint of young women who wanted to marry.

who had misbehaved might be a carry-over from this tradition of the "wild armies." In a sermon on St. Nicholas Day in 1527, Luther rejected this aspect of the Nicholas tradition and stressed instead the image of Nicholas as a bringer of gifts to children. In 1532 Luther penned a statement specifically identifying the figure of St. Nicholas with the Christ child. According to Luther, while children were asleep St. Nicholas came by night to distribute gifts either by lowering them through the chimney

Next on the Luther Christmas calendar was St. Nicholas Day, December 6. In earlier centuries the figure of Nicholas was sometimes associated with pagan rituals. According to one tradition, on December 6, armies of damned souls were released from hell to roam the earth and torment the wicked. The figure of Ruprecht who often accompanied the good bishop to punish children

or by depositing them in empty shoes left outside the door. In an interpretation of Psalm 147, Luther amplifies this attribute of St. Nicholas as a bringer of gifts in the name of the Christ child.

Importantly, Luther reidentified St. Nicholas with the giving of gifts. In many areas of Germany at the time, Nicholas had become associated with varying aspects of pagan personifications of the season of winter. Such a character still lives on today in isolated parts of Germany where he carries the title *Strohnickel* or *Pelznickel*.

Luther also used the image of Nicholas as a gift giver to criticize his clerical contemporaries, charging that some of the then ruling bishops were behaving like "perennial Nicholas bishops." They were using their clerical offices to buy influence. On a few occasions he even used the name *Nickel* or *Schwarzer Nickel* (black Nicholas) to characterize a local diocesan overseer as one who acted out the role not of a bishop but of the devil himself.

The post-Reformation image of St. Nicholas acquired from Luther two separate characteristics that developed in later centuries in opposite directions. On the one hand, St. Nicholas as the gift bearer faded from Thuringia and eventually from the whole of Protestant Germany. His traditional duties were taken over by the character Ruprecht. On the other hand, Luther adopted the folk beliefs about Ruprecht as a helper, not any longer to Nicholas, but to the Christ child who was the sole bringer of gifts.

There are those who credit Luther with initiating the tradition of Christmas bonfires, which still illuminate some central German communities around December 21. Students at Wittenberg University first ignited a huge bonfire in mid-December 1520 to burn the papal law books. This was followed by a torchlight procession in which a straw figure of the pope was set ablaze and carried through the streets of Wittenberg. Although there is historical evidence that this incident actually occurred on December 10th of that year, the traditional bonfire probably is much older, extending all the way back to pagan times. The German tribes all observed a ceremony of lights during the dark nights preceding the winter solstice.

Some sources suggest that in Luther's time adults exchanged gifts not at Christmas (which was more for children) but on New Year's Day. Other sources indicate that Luther, in fact, may have been instrumental in shifting the giving of gifts away from the feast of St. Nicholas on December 6 to the figure of the Christ child on December 25 and that this may have occurred for the first time at Christmas in 1531. Following Luther's preference in this regard, Protestant clergy more and more prescribed that the Christ child and Christmas Day be commemorated with gift giving. By 1570 cities such as Strassburg officially forbade St. Nicholas parades in order to induce children to associate the receiving of gifts with the Christ child. Commonly the Child appeared as a female figure. In post-Reformation years, it was this female child holding a globe who became a folk figure in Christmas Day parades, completely supplanting St. Nicholas.

In the Roman Catholic areas of Germany several traditions persist which Luther tried specifically to suppress. He found that the celebration of midnight mass had a tendency to place too much emphasis on the magical, the heathen, and the spooky aspects of the midnight hour. The midnight mass also included too many carnival-like plays. The belief that young girls would learn the identity of their future husbands during midnight mass also was considered far-fetched. In one of his table talks Luther discouraged not only these practices but also certain folk beliefs (for example, that domestic animals could speak in tongues on Christmas Eve and even predict the future). While some of these superstitions did diminish in response to Luther's suggestions, the custom of feeding the horses and cattle an extra portion on Christmas Eve is still alive, especially in the Roman Catholic regions of Central Europe.

In some sections of Germany, notably in Catholic Austria, midnight mass celebrations were embellished with candlelight processions whose origins reach back to pagan times. This tradition, still common in Alpine districts, incorporated folk beliefs about "wild armies" mentioned earlier in connection with St. Nicholas. In some communities these armies consisted of damned souls returning, in others the armies were made up of witches, in still others they consisted of legions of devils. In several letters to fellow clergy during this time, Luther discouraged this practice but not always successfully as the custom was too deeply seated in the folkloric traditions of the Germans. Carry-overs of the tradition today are the *Sternwallfahrt* (candle or starlight pilgrimage) otherwise known as the *Lichterporzession* (parade of lights) in which people gather at a foreordained site for a candlelight procession to the Roman Catholic churches of Southern Germany and Austria for midnight mass.

Common in the churches of Central European Christendom during Luther's time was the custom of *Kindleinwiegen* (rocking the cradle of the Christ child). In sermons in the years 1525, 1533, and 1535 Luther cautioned his listeners not to allow this holy tradition to take on the carnival atmosphere of the pre-Lenten masquerades. Respectfully executed, however, the tradition was enthusiastically favored by Luther who confirmed his pleasure in it by composing his affectionate Christmas hymn, "*Vom Himmel hoch, da komm ich her.*"

*A*s the "cradle rock" grew ever more embellished in certain districts, Christmas dances developed as an accretion to the once pious practice. In Franconia the dances became an integral part of the midnight mass, which were authorized by the Roman Catholic clergy as a means for the peasants to express their joy surrounding the birth of the Christ child. Sometimes called the *Lobtanz* (dance of praise), the tradition is considered very old in rural Germany. In Thuringia, Hesse, and other states where the dances often were enacted in front of the church on a town square, the practice goes back at least to the Middle Ages (as early as the 13th century) when minnesangers produced versions. Subsequent excesses led to regulation and occasionally to prohibition of the *Lobtanz* in certain cities long before Luther's time. Quite likely, the dances acquired during Luther's life a festival character that went beyond their original basis and intent. Due to civil and clerical restrictions, however, the dances were either banned or more closely integrated with the ceremony of the cradle rock inside the church where the atmosphere of the sanctuary caused them to be more subdued.

Although Luther's final position about cradle rocking

is not entirely clear, we do know that he sought to return the custom to the children themselves. A few comments by contemporaries even suggest that Luther tried to remove the cradle rock from the church and establish it exclusively in the home where even the youngest of children could participate. A writer in Cologne in 1581 also implies that the tradition was gradually moved from the church to the home, even in Roman Catholic circles. In place of the cradle rock in the church, some parishes

the religious gathering for the blessing of oats for the horses, traditionally celebrated on St. Stephan's Day, December 26. Ever since pagan times, the horse had played an extremely important role, not only in the production of food but also for defense, and had enjoyed a status above other animals. It was this folk belief that the Christian missionaries to Germany subsumed when they incorporated preferential treatment for the horse into the Christmas celebration. The feast of St. Stephan,

initiated *Turmsingen* (spire caroling) and a new statue of the Christ child on the altar. Resembling the figure in the Christmas parades, this Christ was depicted as a babe holding a globe of the world in his left hand, blessing it with his right. This tradition still lives on in a few German communities.

One custom that Luther specifically discouraged was

martyr and patron saint of horseriders and coachmen, provided a fitting occasion to give thanks for God's special gift of horses. The blessing of horses on St. Stephan's Day is still celebrated in Germany today, not so much as a church festival but as a family and community event.

Luther also was ambivalent about the custom of the *Johannistrunk* (St. John's toast). Celebrated on the Feast of St. John on December 27, the Christian church apparently subsumed a heathen tradition of the Germanic tribes by initiating a religious blessing for wines and special beers that would be used on specific occasions throughout the year. The ceremony extended to secular settings but was primarily a dedication in the home and community. In some communities this "blessed wine" was served throughout the year whenever friends who had long been absent came together again, or when friends or family members were departing from home for an extended period of time (*Freundschafts* and *Abschiedstrunk*). In the few references Luther made to this custom, he implied that the "friendship" and the "good-bye drink" may have occasioned certain excesses.

New Year's Day was not yet universally celebrated during the time of Luther. Several differing calendars still vied for general acceptance. According to his table talk for January 1, 1539, Luther considered New Year's Day to be somewhat like the feasts of St. Nicholas and Christmas, stressing the giving of gifts primarily to children. He suggested that house servants and farmhands also should share in the exchanges. On several occasions

Luther refers to the exchange of gifts by adults on New Year's Day. On numerous occasions he also referred in his own time to a carnival atmosphere that surrounded this commemoration of the New Year. While he tolerated the revelry in the community he discouraged the excessive practice of tomfoolery inside the churches. Apparently the profane celebration of New Year's Eve inside

the churches began in France during the 10th century and had become rather excessive in Germany during Luther's time. None of this foolishness had any place in a church, according to Luther.

The last of the Christmas holidays on which Luther commented specifically was the feast of the three kings on December 6. On the day before Epiphany in 1531 Luther outlined what he found unacceptable in the celebration of the visitation of the Magi. In the first place he wanted to lay emphasis on celebrating the baptism of Christ, rather than on this visit by the Wise Men about whom so little historical fact is known. Luther found it offensive that children paraded in the streets (*Sternsinger*) bearing lanterns in the shape of stars. He rejected specifically the heavy embellishment of the three kings tradition, which had become grotesquely exaggerated when the supposed relics of their bodies were discovered. According to history, Emperor Friedrich Barbarossa discovered the tombs of the kings near Milan and had them transported in the reliquary built specially for them to the cathedral at Cologne in 1162 where, incidentally, the richly wrought reliquary can still be seen.

In the opinion of Luther, the tradition of the *Sternsinger* rested all too exclusively on ancient Germanic pagan rituals. The parades of the people stressing the regality of the three kings was quite unfitting for a commemoration of the simple birth of the Christ child. Nevertheless, the *Sternsinger* tradition continues in both Catholic and Protestant communities within central Europe. Although less explicit, Luther also toned down the emphasis on lights for the celebration of Candlemas on February 2. In many regions of Germany the Christmas season is not really over before that date, the Feast of the Purification of the virgin mother. Undoubtedly the term Candlemas (*Lichtmess*, in German) likewise was an accommodation of the early missionaries to an ancient Germanic tradition of lights. Scholars usually associate the lights, in some communities commemorated by parades of young men carrying oil-soaked straw torches, with a pre-Christian rite of spring. In the maritime regions of Northern Germany the ceremony was prominent among sailors and seagoing merchants. Torchlight and starlight in the mind of Luther placed too much emphasis on the pre-Christian and superstitious character of the feast and too little on the uniquely simple gift of God in the birth of the Christ child.

Luther's true views on the celebration of Christmas are stated in his sermons on the nativity. They focused on the miraculous birth stripped of all pageantry. With utterly simple diction the reformer communicated the profound theology found in the Christmas story:

How unobtrusively and simply do these events take place on earth that are so heralded in heaven. . . . Behold Christ lying in the lap of his young mother. What can be sweeter than the babe, what more lovely than the mother! What fairer than her youth! What more gracious than her virginity! Look at the child, knowing nothing. Yet all that is belongs to him, that your conscience should not fear but take comfort in him. Doubt nothing! Now is overcome the power of sin, death, hell, conscience and guilt. . . . Believe that he is come, not to judge but to save you.

Pageantry

GRACIA GRINDAL

It's Mary's song of how the mighty fall.
Her small voice quavers through the waiting church.
a little girl in blue with shiny foil
halo around her head. She makes her speech
in words that comprehend what she cannot
before the bathrobed shepherds kneeling there.
The proud shall be brought low. She gets it right.
Suddenly overhead a neon star,
a baby cries, the congregation smiles.
The pantomime of life before us works.
They act the story out, the miracle
becomes them. Rulers have not seen the likes
of this before: cattle, wisemen kneel;
the make-believe before us is made real.

Good News of Great Joy

STEPHEN O. SWANSON

The angel said to the shepherds, "Be not afraid; for behold, I bring you good news of great joy which will come to all the people." When the shepherds returned from the Bethlehem stable praising God for all they had seen and heard, they became forerunners of a gigantic endeavor to tell the good news concerning Christ the Lord. At first the story spread verbally from person to person. Later it was recorded in writing, then laboriously hand copied and preserved in small Christian communities.

It was, however, the invention of the printing press and the almost simultaneous concern of Martin Luther that the good news be made available in the language of the people that sent the angel message soaring to a far broader audience. To continue the publication of the good news has been the dream and the life work of devout people from many nations and generations. Organized into Bible societies, these people have set as their goal: Let everyone hear of the mighty works of God in his or her own language.

The societies have done amazingly well. Around the turn of the 19th century, just before the American Bible Society was begun, the Bible or parts of it had been trans-

lated into over 70 of the world's dialects and languages. Most recently, the society reports that at least one book of the Bible had been translated into 1710 languages and dialects: over 500 in Africa, over 430 in Asia, and over 60 in North America.

The Bible is now available in the languages of 98% of the world's people. But the work is not finished. In the remaining 2% of the world's population around 1400 languages and dialects are left for Bible translators to master.

The Bible societies are involved not only with different languages, but also with different kinds of translations to fill special needs and achieve special goals. The literacy translations, for instance, are designed specifically as reading texts or learning tools for new readers. These texts feature short passages of Scripture that have been translated into a very common and simple language. Although geared for adult learners, these texts can be adapted quite easily for use by children.

Imagine a classroom full of men and women struggling to learn to read. Imagine them studying these specially selected and specially translated texts from the Bible. The heady, moment-by-moment thrill of learning to read their own (or a second) language is mixed with the eter-

This ancient Armenian gospels manuscript (c. 14th-15th century) features a preliminary quire, a sequence of illustrations on the life of Christ. The two pages pictured show the annunciation and the nativity. The world's first Christian kingdom, Armenia was evangelized at the end of the third century. In the fifth century, Mesrop devised an alphabet for Armenian, and then translated the Bible. His translation remains the Armenian standard today.

nal thrill of biblical truth—the good news of Jesus' birth, a miracle of Jesus, or one of his parables. These wonderful stories in a common, simple language are absorbed by eager minds learning a new and important skill. This is the special challenge of the literacy translation.

The idyllic picture of people eagerly learning to read through Bible stories has not been typical of the history of Bible translations, however, and is not even typical everywhere today. (Consider, for instance, the international controversy over Bibles being smuggled into China.) The history of Bible translation and distribution is one of misunderstanding and struggle and persecution, even martyrdom.

In the history of the English language Bible alone the early years were spotted with controversy and persecution that, perhaps, can be exemplified by three of the earliest translators: Wycliffe, Tyndale, and Coverdale. They were neither the first nor the last to suffer for the sake of the Bible, but they typify for us the running battle with established churches and political forces.

John Wycliffe (1320-1384) was not martyred, but he was persecuted severely for his translations as well as for his efforts to reform both church and people. Twenty years after his death, because his influence had continued to grow, Wycliffe's body was dug up and burned and his ashes scattered in a river.

William Tyndale (1494-1536) was martyred. Betrayed by a "friend," imprisoned, and condemned for heresy, Tyndale was then strangled to death and his body was burned. He deserves, perhaps more than anyone else, to be called the father of the English Bible.

England proved itself an inhospitable place for those who first attempted to put the Bible into the hands of the people. Tyndale found refuge from persecution in his homeland by seeking out Luther and Germany. He went to Wittenberg in 1524 and registered at Luther's university there. Tyndale's translation of the Bible was heavily influenced by Luther's ideas and Luther's German translation. It was a simple, people's language Bible that eventually enjoyed some popularity. The life story of Tyndale is fascinating reading. As a man of great energy and passion for spreading the good news to his people, Tyndale soon found himself involved not only in all aspects of the fledgling printing industry in Germany, but also in both open and secret distribution of English Bibles, which were printed on the continent but sold in England.

The Tyndale Bible was prohibited, banned, and burned. One strange story of those times suggests that something of a Bible burning competition took place among English bishops during the reign of Henry VIII. Apparently the Bishop of London wasn't too successful in searching out contraband Tyndale Bibles, so through intermediaries the bishop contacted Tyndale in Germany and bought enough new Bibles for a good

bonfire. Tyndale, however, used the money gained to print even more copies of a newer and better translation.

It wasn't until Thomas Cromwell began to put Protestant ideas into King Henry VIII's mind that an English translation of the Bible was even tolerated. That toleration coincided with the life and work of Miles Coverdale (1488-1569). Coverdale had an up and down career. He started out as a priest but left the orders to become a secular preacher. His English translation was written and printed while he was in Germany during the reign of Henry VIII.

While Cromwell, and hence King Henry, merely tolerated Coverdale and permitted his Bible, Edward the VI actually befriended him, made him his personal chaplain, and later Bishop of Exeter. Edward's successor, Queen Mary, however, persecuted and imprisoned Coverdale. King Christian of Denmark, whose chaplain was Coverdale's brother, interceded with Mary, and Coverdale was allowed to leave England. He went first to Denmark, then back to Germany where he had done his translation in the first place. Coverdale's 81 years spanned several English monarchies and political power struggles in England. He lived long enough to return to England at last during the reign of Queen Elizabeth and often preached in London. He continued to use his title of bishop, though he never again returned to Exeter.

The King James Version (KJV) of 1611 was the beloved Scripture of English speaking peoples for nearly 300 years. It is still the only version accepted by many denominations. So musical and rhythmical and picturesque was it that from time to time it was tuned up but never extensively revised. Like the plays of its contemporary, William Shakespeare, it could hardly be improved upon for its time. The version was named for King James I who authorized and encouraged the translation.

The King James Version began with a conference in 1604 at which 54 learned men were selected to work on the translation. It was to be based on the Bishop's Bible

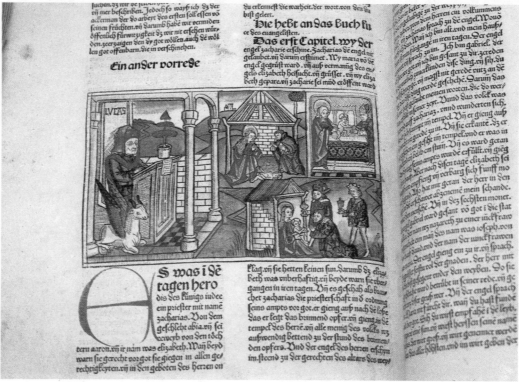

Positioned in the first chapter of Luke, this illustration shows the evangelist Luke and several nativity scenes. This Bible, printed by Anton Koberger of Nuremberg in 1483, was the ninth German Bible to be printed. Colorful illustrations like this, picturing biblical events, appear throughout the volume.

The thirst for the Scriptures is dramatically illustrated in this English Bible dated 1619-1620. A chain fastened the Bible to a lectern or table, to prevent it from being stolen by those eager to read and study God's Word. This King James Version features a stamped leather cover with brass studs.

each other or other authorities to get the best and most sensible translation. The results were spectacular.

The King James Bible was still enjoying its newness, just barely off the presses, when the *Mayflower* landed on American shores in 1620. The Bible—especially the Geneva Bible—sustained these new settlers with the hope and confidence that God would also be with them in this new and wild and unsettled land.

Great Britain maintained a monopoly on Bibles sold in America. It saw the American colonies as a source of raw materials—and as a market for manufactured goods. Bibles, like other commodities, were produced in England and sold in America. Even those English Bibles printed in Germany and the Netherlands almost always were consigned through England. America had no source of its own.

The "shot heard round the world" shot out from under colonial Christians the source of their Bibles. Furthermore, during the War of Independence and for some time after, there was no type, no paper, and no binding material suitable for Bibles anywhere in the colonies. Bibles were terribly scarce. The situation was even debated in Congress in 1777.

Finally in 1782, Robert Aitken, a Philadelphia printer, published the first complete English Bible in America. It was small, 3½ by 6 inches, and hardly beautiful or well-crafted by English standards, but it was American. For collectors today, the little Aitken Bibles are among the most prized and valuable of all English language Bibles.

Out of this scarcity, this famine of Bibles in the new nation, grew the American Bible Society. Founded in 1816 by Elias Boudinot, a former president of the Continental Congress, its name appeared on over 6000 Bibles printed and sold that very year.

The American Bible Society seemed to grow and rise to the needs of the growing nation. It recognized and met needs for special translations for the Indians, for the French in the Louisiana Territory, for the Spanish in Florida and the Southwest. There followed translations for thousands of early immigrants from many countries in Europe: Germany, Scandinavia, Portugal, to name just a few.

By the 1850s new translations were developed for the Chinese immigrating to the West Coast, for Italians, Russians, Poles, Hungarians, and Czechs coming to America. Bilingual editions of the Bible were instrumental in helping these newcomers learn the language of their adopted homeland.

The American Bible Society has been innovative in getting the good news into the hands of people. Their techniques varied from a massive campaign, called General Supply, in the 19th century to support of individuals (called colporteurs) who distributed Bibles one by one on the streets in the new frontiers.

Bibles and New Testaments have been made available to military per-

(1568), which had roots reaching back to the Tyndale Bible and to Coverdale's translation. The KJV was to have no marginal notes (the source of theological controversy), and the translators were encouraged to consult

Both of the translations pictured below are from the Far East, and both show excerpts of the Christmas gospel from Luke 2. Tamil (top) is the language of sections of India and Sri Lanka. Urdu (bottom) is spoken by people who live in areas of Pakistan and India.

sonnel in every war since they were first supplied to the crew of the *John Adams* in 1817. The introduction of Penny Portions in the 1920s, pamphlets containing a single gospel or some other section of Scripture, made for very wide distribution and left the Society's files full of letters from people whose lives were changed by these little bits of the Bible.

The Bible Societies have not limited their distribution to this country. The work has continued nationwide and worldwide with energy, vigor, and innovation. Typical of the ways the Society analyzes and deals with problems was their early discovery that tropical insects loved the glue in Bible bindings. After rejecting the idea of adding poison (imagine a child sucking on the cover of a Bible during a church service), they solved the problem by mixing into their glue large quantities of red pepper.

The nonprofit American Bible Society, in its century-and-a-half existence, has distributed over three billion copies of the Scriptures. Over 80 denominations include the Society as a line item in their annual budgets. The organization now numbers around 30,000 volunteer members.

One of its most recent success stories was the authorizing and publishing of the new translation called *Good News for Modern Man,* one in a series of "common language" translations now being developed by the American Bible Society. Since its publication in 1966, the *Good News* translation has sold over 60 million copies, the greatest bestseller in American publishing history.

These new translations are catalogued along with thousands of Bibles from past times at the society's New York headquarters. A massive library contains one of the largest collections of printed Bibles in the world. The library comprises some 40,000 volumes of Scripture texts in over 1650 different languages and dialects. Treasured historical volumes are found here: for example, about 450 Bibles published before 1600, a Wycliffe New Testament manuscript from about 1440, a 13th century Latin Vulgate manuscript Bible, Martin Luther's translation, and a copy of the first Bible published in America —a 1663 edition in the Massachusetts dialect of the Algonquin Indians. Here, too, one can find the good news of Jesus' birth printed in languages from every continent: in Urdu from India, in Grebo from Liberia, in Cherokee from the United States, in Tagalog from the Philippines, in Frisian from the Netherlands, in Tumbalá Chol from Mexico. The library continues to grow as more and more translations are made.

The "good news of great joy" proclaimed by the angels on that first Christmas night will be read this Christmas season by millions upon millions of people. All over the world, families will gather to read that joyous message—"To you is born a Savior"—each in their own language.

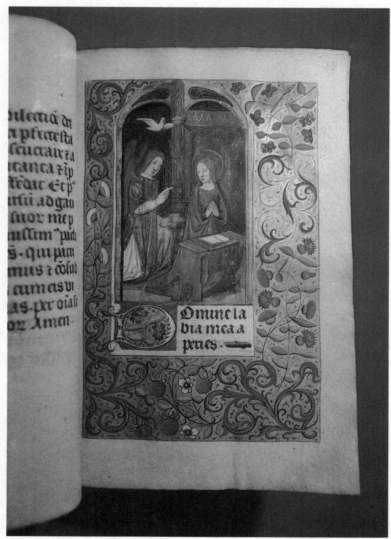

This beautifully illustrated and decorated page from a Latin Book of Hours pictures the annunciation. The style is typical of artists in the south Netherlands (now Belgium) of the mid-15th century. A book of hours was a personal prayerbook which included scripture readings and devotional material.

Cree, an American Indian language, was reduced to a syllabic system of writing in about 1840 by missionary James Evans. He not only invented the characters, but he also cut the first type. A segment of Luke 2 is shown (left). An excerpt from a Japanese translation of John 1 is pictured at right.

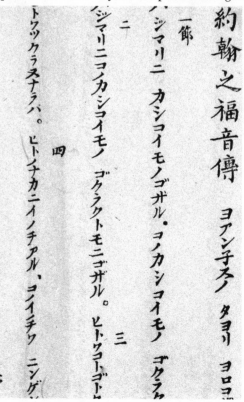

Nativity

Parement Master, c. 1382

PHILLIP GUGEL

Painted by an anonymous artist, now known as the "Parement Master," and his shop, this elaborate manuscript illumination is a page from the *Très Belles Heures de Notre Dame* (Most Beautiful Hours of Our Lady), a book of hours commissioned by John, Duke of Berry. Its design unites four types of medieval book illumination: a full miniature, an historiated initial, a *bas de page* (bottom of the page) scene, and a decorated border.

The Parement Master—named after his major work, the *Parement de Narbonne*, an altar frontal owned by the Louvre—painted Mary lying on a cushion as she adores her son. This had been her posture in nativity scenes since the Byzantine era. Then, due to St. Bridget's and St. Bernard's influence, artists showed her in rapt adoration. The two traditions of depicting Mary are combined here.

Another influence from Byzantine art, the infant's tomblike manger, stands before Mary, on her right. Only the Christ child wears a cruciform halo, or nimbus. His blessing to his parents symbolizes his divine calling, which they humbly acknowledge.

Joseph, traditionally shown as a bearded, elderly man, devotedly watches over his family. Their elegant, graceful figures are characteristic of those in late 14th century French illumination.

Because the figures of the holy family dominate the miniature, the Parement Master had to reduce the size of their surroundings. The stable is merely a thatched canopy, providing minimal shelter, and it is doubtful Mary and Joseph could stand under it. In the foreground, the ass and ox are only the size of large dogs!

The two sections of wickerwork fence, a common device of late Gothic painting, are an attempt to establish spatial boundaries and a sense of recession. In a similar way, the small stylized hills with their sparse foliage are a backdrop for the holy family and effect some background spatial recession. The Parement Master was not very successful in his attempts to achieve this.

If you look carefully, you will see that the dark blue evening sky is filled with the nimbused heads of angels. Those under the stable roof are holding a banderole, or scroll, which bears a Latin inscription of their song of praise: "Glory to God in the highest."

The gold border that frames the miniature is an indication that the Parement Master probably was a panel painter as well as a manuscript illuminator.

The historiated *D* initial sets off several lines of the hand-lettered medieval Latin text for the hour of Prime, one of the monastic liturgical services. Books of hours associated this service with Christ's nativity. An historiated initial has a small picture around or within it. Here, the *D* initial contains a colorfully garbed angel with a scroll. It contains the opening words of the message to the shepherds. Besides its pictorial purpose, the initial connects two sections of foliate scrolls on the left border, and serves as a transitional decoration from the full miniature to the text and the shepherds' scene.

One of the Master's pupils might have painted this scene, since the blocky, dwarflike shepherd figures lack the graceful proportions of the holy family. However, each of them has a different pose; the one on the left with his head thrown back as he gazes at the angel is particularly amusing. They are dressed like medieval peasants. Two of them lean on their *houlettes* (a hooked staff with a shovel at one end). Although the annunciation to the shepherds traditionally took place at night, only the angel in the *D* initial is shown against a dark sky. The dog and sheep in their rigidly profiled ranks are toylike, though the ones watching the angel are a bit more animated. Little attention was paid to the landscape's depth and scale due to its position. The minuscule hills, with their mushroomlike trees, cannot provide a sense of spaciousness. The bagpipe held by the seated shepherd is his traditional attribute.

The border's stylized ivy leaves are one of the most characteristic features of full-page illuminations in books of hours from the late 14th and early 15th centuries. Between the ivy vines, half-length angels hold banderoles inscribed with words from the Christmas gospel. Since the owl was a bird of ill omen in traditional iconography, its presence in the bottom border is an odd detail. The border completes and adds interest to the illuminated design.

A book of hours was a personal prayerbook for the laity that combined portions of the services appointed for the daily worship of monastic communities with materials of a more personal or secular nature. Since these books of hours were not regulated by the clergy, they sometimes had curious additions, such as a prayer against bedbugs!

Not only was a book of hours a devotional aid; owning a book like the *Très Belles Heures* was a status symbol. Such a book was acquired for its fine art and for the prestige it gave. Since the edges of this illumination show no wear, it is doubtful that Duke John used it for prayer.

As an example of manuscript illumination from the royal court of France, the Parement Master's *Nativity* delights our eyes and in its own way proclaims: "Glory to God in the highest."

A Family Christmas

BOB ARTLEY

The iron runners slid and bumped over the snow-packed roads, rumbled over wooden bridges, and screeched, cold steel on cold steel, over the railroad crossings. The horses pulled the bobsled with ease and I was glad. I liked riding, and I didn't want to think of the horses having a hard time of it for my fun. Dolly and Daisy had pulled us along in the sled for about 12 miles. I did wonder about the horses' feet. Were they as cold as mine?

We all— Mom, Dad, my brother, and I— had been made snug for the journey when we left home early that afternoon. However, by now the cold had begun to seep through our heavy wraps. Frost was forming on the scarf that covered the lower part of my face. My fingers, in the double layered mittens, were tingling with the cold. But worst of all, my toes felt like small frozen potatoes in the front end

of my booted shoes. I was sure they would spill out of my socks when I undressed them.

Suddenly the discomforts of the lengthy, open-air ride were forgotten. Over a rise in the snowy landscape appeared the familiar, long, tree-lined lane that led to Grandma's and Grandpa's farmstead. We were going there for Christmas!

By the time our bobsled pulled up in front of the houseyard gate, Grandpa was on the porch pulling on his coat, and cousins appeared at the windows. The next few moments were pandemonium. We boys were out of the bobsled and up the freshly shoveled walk to be hugged by Grandpa and Grandma, then into the fragrant warmth of Grandma's kitchen to be greeted by the rest.

Grandpa helped Dad put Dolly and Daisy into the stall in the barn and gave them a generous portion of oats and timothy hay— their Christmas dinner.

And what a dinner was being prepared for us in Grandma's kitchen!

After our wraps had been put away and the kisses had been wiped from our cheeks (Mom's family was generous in its show of affection), we cousins went whooping through the house, anxious to view the gaily decorated Christmas tree in the parlor. A huge pile of brightly wrapped packages lay beneath its fragrant branches.

Then we flew back through the living room (where we were asked to slow down by Uncle George), around the stretched-out table with its festive setting in the dining room, and on into the kitchen to the source of those wonderful aromas.

Grandma was supervising everything. Mom and my aunts were helping with the last-minute details. There were pumpkin pies and a big bowl of whipped cream. (A surreptitious sample on the tip of the finger revealed it to be flavored with just the right amount of vanilla.) There were pickles (sliced cucumber, beet, and spiced crab apple), freshly baked buns, mashed potatoes, creamed carrots, and a large casserole of scalloped corn. Central to the whole feast was the huge turkey, beautifully browned. Grandma had just pulled it from the oven. The dressing was scooped into a serving dish and the gravy prepared.

Word was passed around that everyone should come to the table. We needed no coaxing and the whole family was soon seated on dining chairs, kitchen chairs, the piano bench, and a kitchen stool around that groaning oak table. My brother, Dean,

the youngest and smallest, had to sit on the huge family Bible placed on his chair to bring him up to table height. Grandpa remarked that Dean wouldn't go wrong if he always used it as his foundation. Then we all bowed our heads for Grandpa's prayer of thanksgiving. Indeed, there was much to be thankful for.

When our hunger was appeased, our thoughts turned to the Christmas tree set in front of the west window in the parlor. It was somewhat spindly, but its fragrance made up for its appearance. The base of this green spruce was set in a bucket of wet sand, and this in turn was covered by a white sheet.

An impressive assortment of gaily colored tissue wrapped packages was piled high under the branches of the tree. A little tag was attached to each package, designating for whom it was intended and from whom it came. Up in the branches nestled

smaller packages and other decorations— colored glass balls, bits of tinsel, and colored paper cones filled with popcorn, peanuts, and hard candies. At the very top of the tree was a cardboard star covered with lead foil.

By the time dinner was over, the grey sky outside had turned to black and the kerosene lamps needed to be lit. While the table was cleared, leftovers put into the pantry, the dishes washed, and the milking done, we kids tried to contain our excitement in anticipation of the gift exchange. The time dragged on and we were told repeatedly to quiet down. Aunt Ethel tried, without success, to steer us into quiet, sitting games.

Finally the last dish was put away, the milk from the barn was strained and put into crocks to cool in the pantry, and everyone began to gather in the parlor. It was decided that Cousin Verl would read

the tags on the packages and we smaller ones would deliver them to the persons intended.

It was a noisy, exciting time. Grandma and Grandpa were more or less accorded a place of honor, and everyone took note of the gifts they received. It was like a multi-ring circus as everyone opened and exclaimed over their gifts.

The gifts were simple, practical things for the most part, but they seemed luxurious to us. There were brightly colored mittens of intricate design that Grandma had spent many hours knitting for the whole family. Those for the younger ones were tied together with a yarn string to keep them from becoming separated and lost. Grandpa had made spinning tops from wooden

spools for thread. There were also purchased gifts—toys, slippers, scarves, shawls, delicate dishes, vases, and books— it seemed there were books for everyone.

After the last gift had been unwrapped and the last tissue wrapping paper had been either folded carefully (for next year) or stuffed into a cardboard box, Aunt Bertha started playing Christmas carols on the piano. Gradually we all gathered around, making a joyous sound in celebration of the wonderful season.

After the songfest, when things had almost calmed down, Aunt Ethel suggested how nice it would be to have a sleigh ride. The suggestion was met with enthusiasm by everyone but our family. (We had just gotten warm after our long bobsled ride that very afternoon.) Aunt Ethel, Uncle Will, and Cousin Verl were from the city, so to them it

would be a treat. After some persuading by the others, we finally caught the spirit. Dad agreed to reharness Daisy and Dolly and hitch them to the bobsled.

All of us, with the exception of Grandma and Mom, bundled up in our winter wraps and piled on the bobsled. Someone held a lighted kerosene lantern in the front and another held one in the rear. Behind the bobsled, attached by a rope, was a coaster sled on which we smaller cousins took turns riding.

Dad guided the horses in an easy trot across the farmyard and down the long lane. On either side of the lane stood large maple trees whose branches met overhead, making a "covered bridge" in the summertime.

But tonight, the trees' bare branches reached into the cold darkness of the winter night, and the lane was choked with drifts of snow. The drifts weren't large, but they caused an undulating ride in the sled. They also caused the little sled behind to dump its squealing cargo now and then. When this happened the team was stopped, the little sled was set upright and remounted, and we were off again amid much laughing and shouting.

At the end of the lane we turned north onto the road past the farm. Our merry band formed a cozy cocoon of sound and light as we moved through the vast expanse of silence and darkness in the cold winter landscape. Now and then a twinkling light could be seen here and there across the fields and through the groves — silent testimony to life besides ours in this snowy farmland, perhaps also celebrating Christmas.

We drove past the crossroads for about a half mile, then turned into the open gate to a field, cir-

cled back onto the road, and headed south toward home. Before long we were back in the farmyard.

Our jolly band came laughing, puffing, and stomping into the kitchen where Grandma and Mom had prepared a lunch of hot cocoa and leftovers from dinner. During the rest of the evening, the grownups visited, read from their Christmas books, or dozed in their chairs near the warmth of the hardcoal burner. We kids tried out our toys again, and Grandpa read to us from some of our new books.

The old Seth Thomas clock on the shelf in the kitchen "bonged" nine o'clock and bedtime was decreed. We didn't mind, however, for we liked the upstairs in this old house. We climbed the stairway where we had spent hours bouncing rubber balls. The four bedrooms opening off the hallway were excellent for playing "bear," a scary version of hide and seek. In the small northeast bedroom a door led to the attic, which contained all sorts of interesting things.

We were to sleep in the southeast room in a big black walnut bed— large and sturdy enough to accommodate three lively boys who had to be reminded repeatedly to get to sleep.

Eventually, after the kerosene lamp was placed in the hall beyond our open door, things did quiet down and I became aware of the measured breathing of Dean and Harold.

As I became more and more drowsy, I heard the groaning of the windmill outside and the comforting sound of muffled voices from downstairs. Finally, the Seth Thomas down in the kitchen began to strike the hour of ten. I didn't hear it finish.

The Animals of Christmas

BETTY HARMON

Christ was born in an enclosure, possibly a cave, used to shelter animals. His first bed was a manger, an oblong troughlike wooden box from which animals fed. Because the population of Bethlehem had suddenly multiplied with the influx of families who were there to be counted in the Roman census, this was the only shelter Mary and Joseph could find.

At that time many kept their valuable animals sheltered under the same roof as the family, separated by only a wall. So the nearness of animals to a family was not as unusual as we think today. But the hasty arrangement Joseph made with the Bethlehem innkeeper seems to have been for makeshift housing in quarters actually occupied by animals and appropriated in an emergency. So the Scriptures say: "(Mary) brought forth her firstborn son, and wrapped him in swaddling clothes, and laid him in a manger" (Luke 2:7).

Through the years, as the birth of Christ has been celebrated, legends have sprung up about animals and Christ's birth in a stable. The tellers of these stories have given to the animals of Christmas the highest human motivations. These legends are told in the Christmas carols and poems of many nations.

A traditional French-Canadian carol, "Whence Art Thou, My Maiden," has this exquisite lyric:

I saw ass and oxen, kneeling meek and mild,
With their gentle breathing warm the holy Child.

Ox and ass are also included in William Morris' French carol, "Masters in this Hall":

Ox and ass him know,
Kneeling on their knee,
Wondrous joy had I
This little babe to see.

This same thought is lifted to sublime heights and linked to the angels in Christina Rosetti's lovely hymn/poem, "In the Bleak Midwinter":

Enough for him, whom angels
Fall down before,
The ox and ass and camel
Which adore.

Many generations in every country grew up with the legend of animals in the stable kneeling in homage at the birth of Jesus Christ, God's holy Son. A 16th century carol, "With Merry Heart," describes the scene:

Both ox and ass, adoring in the byre,
In mute acclaim pay homage to our Sire.

Thomas Hardy, the English novelist and poet, wrote a poem about this legend.

Christmas Eve, and twelve of the clock.
    "Now they are all on their knees,"
An elder said as we sat in a flock
    By the embers in hearthside ease.

We pictured the meek mild creatures where
    They dwelt in their strawy pen,
Nor did it occur to one of us there
    To doubt they were kneeling then.

But in the final stanzas of "The Oxen," Hardy laments that such a lovely story is no longer given credence.

So fair a fancy few would weave
    In these years! Yet, I feel,
If someone said on Christmas Eve,
    "Come; see the oxen kneel

In the lonely barton by yonder coomb (valley)
    Our childhood used to know."
I should go with him in the gloom,
    Hoping it might be so.

As we read these wistful words, we are glad that "so fair a fancy" has been woven in times past and still has the power to stir our imaginations.

One of the oldest and best-loved songs about the animals of Christmas is the 12th century English carol, "The Friendly Beasts."

Jesus our brother, kind and good,
Was humbly born in a stable rude,
And the friendly beasts around him stood;
Jesus our brother, kind and good.

In subsequent stanzas, each beast tells of the part he played in the birth of Christ: the donkey carried Mary, his mother, to Bethlehem; the cow gave her manger for his bed; the sheep gave wool for a blanket; the dove cooed him to sleep.

Thus every beast by some good spell,
In the stable dark was glad to tell
Of the gift he gave Emmanuel,
The gift he gave Emmanuel.

The prophet Isaiah uses animals to picture the peaceable kingdom of the Righteous One:

The wolf shall dwell with the lamb,
and the leopard shall lie down with the kid,
and the calf and the lion and the fatling together,
and a little child shall lead them.

Masters in This Hall

William Morris

French
arr. Robert J. Powell

1. Mas - ters in this hall, Hear ye news to - day
2. Shep - herds man - y an one Sat a - mong the sheep,
3. Shep - herds should of right Leap and dance and sing,
4. "How name ye this lord, Shep-herds?" then said I,

Brought from o - ver sea, And ev - er I you pray:
No man spake more word Than they had been a - sleep:
Thus to see ye sit Is a right strange thing:
"Ver - y God," they said, "Come from heav - en high":

No - el! No - el! No - el! No - el sing we clear! Holp - en

are all folk on earth, Born is God's Son so dear:

No - el! No - el! No - el! No - el sing we loud! God to-

day hath poor folk raised And cast a - down the proud.

5. Therein did we see
   A sweet and goodly may
   And a fair old man,
   Upon the straw she lay:

6. Ox and ass him know,
   Kneeling on their knee,
   Wondrous joy had I
   This little babe to see:

In the Bleak Midwinter

Christina Rossetti

Gustav Holst
arr. John Seagard

1. In the bleak mid-win-ter Frost-y wind made
2. Our God, heav'n can-not hold him Nor earth sus-
3. E-nough for him, whom che-ru-bim Wor-ship night and

moan, Earth stood hard as i-ron, Wa-ter like a
tain; Heav'n and earth shall flee a-way When he comes to
day, A breast-ful of milk And a man-ger-ful of

stone; Snow had fal-len, snow on snow, Snow on snow,
reign: In the bleak mid-win-ter A sta-ble-place suf-ficed The
hay; E-nough for him, whom an-gels Fall down be-fore, The

In the bleak mid-win-ter, Long a-go.
Lord God Al-might-y Je-sus Christ.
ox and ass and ca-mel Which a-dove.

4. Angels and archangels
May have gathered there,
Cherubim and seraphim
Thronged the air:
But only his mother
In her maiden bliss
Worshiped the beloved
With a kiss.

5. What can I give him,
Poor as I am?
If I were a shepherd
I would bring a lamb;
If I were a wise man
I would do my part;
Yet what I can I give him —
Give my heart.

Tune used by permission of Oxford University Press. Setting copyright 1983 Augsburg Publishing House.

The Friendly Beasts

Robert Davis, alt.

Medieval French
arr. Melvin Rotermund

1. Je - sus our broth - er, strong and good, Was
2. "I," said the don - key, shag - gy and brown, "I
3. "I," said the cow, all white and red, "I
4. "I," said the sheep, with curl - y horn, "I

hum - bly born in a sta - ble rude, And the
car - ried his moth - er up hill and down, I
gave him my man - ger for his bed, I
gave him my wool for his blan - ket warm, He

friend - ly beasts a - round him stood,
car - ried her safe - ly to Beth - le - hem town;
gave him my hay to pil - low his head;
wore my coat on Christ - mas morn;

Je - sus our broth - er, strong and good.
I," said the don - key, shag - gy and brown.
I," said the cow, all white and red.
I," said the sheep, with curl - y horn.

5. "I," said the dove, from the rafters high,
"I cooed him to sleep that he should not cry,
We cooed him to sleep, my mate and I;
I," said the dove, from the rafters high.

6. Thus ev'ry beast, by some good spell,
In the stable dark was glad to tell
Of the gift he gave Emmanuel;
The gift he gave Emmanuel.

With Merry Heart

Piae Cantiones, 1582
tr. Maurice F. Bell

Piae Cantiones, 1582
arr. Paul Lohman

1. With mer ~ ry heart let
2. An an ~ gel's voice let de ~
3. The shep ~ herds sped to

all re ~ joice in one; The
clared the Sav ~ ior's birth, The Glo ~
see this won ~ drous thing And

moth ~ er maid hath now brought forth her
ry to God, good ~ will and peace on
found the babe, the which is Christ our

son In Beth ~ le ~ hem.
earth: In Beth ~ le ~ hem.
King: In Beth ~ le ~ hem. hem.

4. Both ox and ass, adoring in the byre,
   In mute acclaim pay homage to our Sire:
   In Bethlehem.

5. Now bless we Christ, eternal glory's King,
   And Christ bless us, as to his praise we sing:
   In Bethlehem.

Text from *The Oxford Book of Carols*, by permission of Oxford University Press.
Setting copyright 1983 Augsburg Publishing House.

Whence Art Thou

Traditional French Canadian
tr. William McLennan

Traditional French Canadian
arr. Normand Lockwood

1. "Whence art thou, my maid-en, whence art thou?"
2. "What saw'st thou, my maid-en, what saw'st thou?"
3. "Noth-ing more, my maid-en, noth-ing more?"

"I come from the sta-ble where, this ver-y night,
"There with-in a man-ger, a lit-tle child I saw
"There I saw the moth-er her sweet ba-by hold,

I, a shep-herd maid-en, saw a won-drous sight."
Ly-ing, soft-ly sleep-ing, on a bed of straw."
And the fa-ther, Jo-seph, trem-bling with the cold."

4. "Nothing more, my maiden, nothing more?
   Nothing more, my maiden, nothing more?"
   "I saw ass and oxen, kneeling meek and mild,
   With their gentle breathing warm the holy child."

5. "Nothing more, my maiden, nothing more?
   Nothing more, my maiden, nothing more?"
   "There were three bright angels come down from the sky,
   Singing forth sweet praises to our God on high."

The Feast of Lights

Christmas in Denmark, Norway, Sweden, and Germany

LA VERN J. RIPPLEY

Like the northern lights, Christmas is a beacon of life-bringing brightness to the lands washed by the North and Baltic Seas.

Christianity arrived late in northern Europe. Missionaries first penetrated only those provinces which belonged to the Roman Empire: Spain, France, the British Isles, and the countries along the Mediterranean. Farther north and east, they did not succeed in spreading the gospel until about the year 1000. Although Charlemagne had facilitated the conversion of southern Germany by his Baptism 200 years earlier and St. Boniface had pushed as far north as the city of Fulda in 754, this was beyond, deep in Germanic pagan territory. East and north of the Elbe River there was no penetration of Christianity until after the first millenium—not until the period of the Crusades brought fighting zeal to the proponents of the Christian tradition. Godfred, the first recorded Danish king, defeated Charlemagne shortly after the year 800, thus preventing Germany and Christianity from expanding north for two centuries. King Harold Bluetooth is credited with establishing the first semblance of Christianity in Denmark about 980.

Even more time was needed for the missionaries to take the news of Christ's birth across the Kattegat and the Skagerrak, the two channels that separate Denmark from the peninsula of Norway and Sweden. King Olaf I of Norway (969-1000) was christened while on an expedition to England and on his return initiated the new religion in Norway. Around 830 Sweden was visited by St. Ansgar (801-865) who arrived from Charlemagne's Germany as the first missionary. But Christianity was neither widespread nor officially accepted until 1008 when Olaf Skottkonung, the ruler of Northern Sweden, was converted from paganism. Thereupon, a civil war erupted in a wave of pagan reaction and foreign invasion with the result that Christianity virtually disappeared until the 12th century. The Swedish King Eric (d. 1160) officially recognized it as the faith of his country, and thereby gained for himself the title of patron saint of Sweden. Many forces aided the spread of Christianity during this time. Of considerable importance was the commercial interaction between German and Scandinavian cities due to the prominence of the Hanseatic League in all cities adjoining the North and Baltic Seas.

In the center of this area lies Denmark. Here the religious spirit had been Protestant, more specifically Lutheran, ever since 1530 when Denmark's Frederick I permitted Lutheran preachers to introduce the Reformation. Many annual festivals, however, still bear resemblances to the Nordic pagan mythology. Easter brings with it the rites of early spring, Whitsun those of late spring. Walpurgis Night with its demons is commemorated during the darkness from April 30 to May 1. Summer feasts of light are widespread during the initial days of summer and many traditions concerning the death and rebirth of light are reenacted during the Christmas season. As in all countries of this watershed, Christmas is the most extensively celebrated season of the year.

The Danish Christmas season begins weeks in advance with preparations for the Advent wreath. The key element in it and almost every other symbolic display or ornament is the candle—candles in wreaths, candles in windows of homes, candles in churches. In Denmark as in all countries of northern Europe, the feast of St. Lucia is celebrated on December 13. While Swedish families enact elaborate ceremonies on this feast of lights, the Danes somberly search the sky at nightfall for the *luzieschien*, a mysterious light which is supposed to reveal the future. Girls hope to discover what lies ahead—and especially whom they will marry. In a few very traditional Danish families young women study the waters of a moonlit brook, while praying that God reveal to them who will be their husbands. Here, too, candles sometimes take the place of the moon.

The children are introduced to the spirit of Christmas by the Advent calendar on which they find small gifts. Everyday the children open a small present until Christmas when the last and most anticipated gift is received.

On December 21, the feast of St. Thomas, Danish school-aged children are allowed to play tricks on their teachers and parents, such as locking them out of the classroom or house. Occasionally they swap roles; the elders write school reports, while the children assume the historical identities of clerics or kings.

Everywhere are decorations or *pynt*, the Danish word for artful arrangements and trimmings for the house and Christmas tree. Usually a tree is procured, cut in the woods if possible, long before Christmas Day. Before the children see it, however, adults decorate it with handmade ornaments of paper or felt in the shapes of angels, birds, apples, hearts, and *nisser* (Christmas elves) plus real candles, which are lighted when the children are permitted to see the tree for the first time.

As if to exemplify their generosity to each other, Danes use hearts as a central theme in all their Christmas decorations: hearts on the Christmas tree, hearts in the form of mobiles for the home and office, hearts as table decorations, baked goods in the form of hearts. Also coming from the heart is the tradition of feeding the birds at Christmastime. As in Norway and Sweden, families place a sheaf of grain on a pole or on the gable of a barn to provide the birds with something special at Christmas.

On Christmas Eve Danes go to church services, which often are scheduled at 4:00 p.m. to allow time for a special dinner and celebrations of the family at home afterward. Baking has been done in advance. Specialties include the *klejner* and *julekage,* marzipan tarts and vanilla wreaths. Red cabbage is a must, as is the traditional roast goose, which is accompanied by *leverpostej,* a liver paste that tastes marvelous on Danish pumpernickel bread. The *julnisse* (elves), who substitute for our Santa Claus, come during the night and, in most families, find a bowl of rice and milk or shares of the Christmas baking left for them outside the door or on the mantel in the living room.

Following dinner, the Danish family proceeds to the Christmas room where all members join hands around the tree and sing traditional carols before opening the

ministrative units: 9 *Bispedommer* (bishoprics), 91 *Prostier* (archdeaconries), and 562 *Prestegjeld* (clerical districts). The clergy are appointed by the king, and both women and men are admissible. Because of geographic and organizational isolation, Norwegian traditions vary greatly from place to place.

Christmas in all of Norway is celebrated with a rich blend of pagan and Christian traditions. Coniferous trees are so plentiful that they grace not only the homes of all Norwegians but also the public buildings and open markets of every city and town. A coastal nation, Norway relies on its fishing industry, so naturally the Christmas tree is carried to the sea. Every Norwegian ship features a Christmas tree on its mast wherever it is during the holy season. Churches, schools, hospitals all enjoy Christmas trees. But the Norwegians do not stop at home; they even send trees as gifts to London, the Hague, Reykjavik (the capital of Iceland), and to continental Euro-

gifts. In Denmark everyone can count on getting something for Christmas because the nation has organized a Christmas lottery to raise funds to buy gifts for the disadvantaged members of the population. It is sponsored by the daily newspapers and offers attractive incentives for all citizens to share with the needy.

In Norway, life and its traditions are conditioned by two powerful forces, one physical, the other spiritual—a rugged, enormously long coastline along the vengeful North Sea and the Evangelical Lutheran state church. Like the nation itself, the church is subdivided into ad-

pean capitals as a sign of Norwegian goodwill during the season of Christmas.

One favorite food of Norwegians at Christmastime is fish, not necessarily *lutefisk* which has become a tradition among the Norwegians in America, but fine fish of one kind or another. *Lutefisk* is, if anything, scorned at home. A 19th century method for drying cod, *lutefisk* even in its heyday was thought to be of mediocre quality. Nevertheless it became a nostalgic delicacy for 19th century Norwegian emigrants and their descendants in America. The *julegrisen* (Christmas pig) is another favorite, yielding all sorts of holiday dishes including the feet which are considered a delicacy when pickled in brine. On occasion rural Norwegians delight in picking apart the pickled pigs' feet as they drink a toast of *brennevin.* Norwegians are also unsurpassed for their fine baked goods in the Christmas season. According to tradition, a homemaker must bake at least seven varieties, preferably 14 or 21 or any multiple of seven.

Rice porridge is standard fare on the traditional Christmas menu. Some families serve it on Christmas Eve with one almond hidden in the entire batch. The lucky person who finds the nut receives a special reward, often a marzipan pig decorated with a red ribbon. On coastal farms in Norway an elfin tenant helper, called *nissen,* is believed to reside in the barn year-round to keep an eye on everything and everybody. His only annual reward is a bowl of the traditional rice porridge on Christmas Eve. But the favor is not one-sided. If the *nissen* empties his

family. In this way they determine what blessings will come to the family members during the next year. Birds are remembered with bountiful sheaves of grain that are posted in the yard or attached to the roofs of buildings in the farmyard. Here, too, the occasion has a prophetic intention: If large numbers of birds come to enjoy the benefits, the next year will be a good one for the farmer.

At about 4:00 p.m. on Christmas Eve, church bells signal the closing of stores, offices, and places of business. Families gather for a Christmas Eve supper, which may be more or less sumptuous depending on plans for feasting on Christmas Day. Usually the Christmas tree is decorated with traditional ornaments, foods, and small Norwegian flags. Santa Claus has no place in the Norwegian scheme of things. His task is done by the *julenissen,* a Christmas elf who has already brought the gifts and placed them under the tree. On Christmas Eve children wait outside for the tree to be trimmed and lighted.

Sweden

bowl, that's a good omen for the farmer as well as for the elf. It means he has a home for the next 12 months. If the bowl is not found empty, it signals trouble for the farmer because the good elf has decided to move elsewhere.

Not only elves but domestic animals—cattle, horses, pigs—all get extra portions on Christmas Eve. According to some traditions, the extra supply of grain and fodder is given several days before Christmas, because on Christmas Eve the animals hold a conference exactly at midnight to discuss their impression of the farmer and his

Or, perhaps, they are sent to visit homes in the neighborhood to extend Christmas wishes in return for fresh-baked cookies or candy.

Following dinner the family gathers in the room with the tree. They join hands and circle the tree, singing the most beloved of Christmas carols—for example, *"Da tender moder alle lys og ingen krok er mørk"* ("Then mother lights the Christmas tree and fills the room with light"). Gifts are passed out and merriment continues until late at night. In rural areas ancestral spirits are thought to visit families at this time. Thus, a goat's head whose horns bear a garland of straw (the symbol of a dead ancestor) is a welcome gift on this occasion. In towns where this kind of gift is now dissociated from its legendary significance, the gift of a goat's head is a simple joke with no reference to ghosts of the past.

In addition to attending church services on Christmas Day, Norwegians visit relatives all day long. On December 26, also a legal holiday in Norway, children in particular enjoy the popular Christmas play, *Reisen til Julestjernen (The Search for the Christmas Star)*, which is staged in numerous theaters throughout the country. The story is a typical fairy tale in which a princess is kidnapped. The king in his sorrow banishes the Christmas star from above his palace. It is found again only when a young girl in rags treks through the forests, speaking with the birds and animals, until a miracle causes the Christmas star to shine again. She carries it to the king, who discovers her to be his long-lost daughter. In the story lies the significance of the star and of light for Norwegians during the Christmas season. Men sometimes wear a star in their buttonholes and star singers sell them on street corners throughout the season. Stars appear again after Christmas in commemoration of the Magi and the celebration of the Epiphany.

Enjoying many similarities with its neighbor to the west, Sweden also has distinct Christmas traditions, many of which derive from the state Lutheran church. During the reign of Gustavus I, Sweden secularized all church property (1527-29) and made Lutheranism the law of the land. This decision had a religious basis but was primarily a device to weaken the Hanseatic League's monopoly in trade. Secularization also served to centralize the power of the crown over the aristocracy in the provinces. At any rate, the Lutheran tradition of worship was firmly anchored in Swedish soil. Sweden is perhaps best remembered for Gustavus II (1594-1632) who made Sweden into a great European power. As a crusader for Lutheranism, he invaded Germany during the Thirty Years' War (1618-1648) and won several brilliant battles before his death in the battle of Lutzen. Although Gustavus died, his opponent, the Catholic General Wallenstein, lost the battle. Thus Lutheranism was established in the whole of Europe including northern Germany.

Perhaps more than any other nation in northern Europe, Sweden has absorbed the traditions and the folklore of the winter solstice into the Christmas season. In rural areas green branches are hung out to remind the farmers of spring. Bundles of oats are hung from rooftops, from poles, or from the decorative greenery. Originally the oats were intended for Odin's horse on his trips to Valhalla but today the birds are the beneficiaries in the dark, snowy Swedish winter. The Christmas season begins not with Advent, nor even with the feast of St. Nicholas as is common in other nations on the Continent, but on December 13. This is the feast of St. Lucia (her name in Latin means "light"), the feast of lights.

The day begins when a youthful daughter serves her parents and siblings Lucia buns and coffee in bed. Wearing a long white gown and a crown of evergreen branches decorated with at least seven lighted candles, this maiden literally and figuratively dispels the darkness from the home. During the day there are processions in the streets, often headed by star-bearing young men. In the evening there are Lucia balls. According to legend, St. Lucia was blinded because she gave her wedding gifts to the poor. When her eyesight was miraculously restored, she was sentenced to be burned at the stake, but the flames refused their prey. In a nation where the winter solstice is so conspicuous, this death-defying personage of light became an appropriate symbol for Christian missionaries teaching the meaning of Christ's birth.

Following the pattern in other Scandinavian lands, there is no St. Nicholas nor Santa Claus. Instead the good elf *jultombe* (Christmas gnome) brings good things for children. They reward his arrival by putting large helpings of Christmas cake out for him to eat. On the farms the *julklapp* is still a tradition. This ceremony calls for families to gather at the windows of their houses and throw out gifts. In the strict tradition these gifts were straw figures of animals, especially horses or people. The practice was supposed to bring good luck to the home and its dwellers. Introduced from Germany during the 19th century, the Christmas tree is today central to the celebration of Christmas in Sweden. Also imported from Sweden's neighbors is the tradition of children dressed in white who go from house to house singing carols in return for candy and slices of Christmas cake.

Most Swedish festivals occur at the changing of the seasons, and special seasonal foods grace the tables on these occasions. At Christmas the Swedes begin on St. Lucia by eating lots of *lussekatter* (saffron cakes). This expands greatly on Christmas Day when the *julbord* (Christmas table) might include pickled elk meat, turkey, rice pudding, and a generous *allmant smörgåsbord* (a buffet of varied hors d'oeuvres). Dried fish, popular among Swedes in the United States and known both here and in Sweden as *lutfish*, is no longer the delicacy in the homeland that it is among emigrant families. Most tables, however, will include varieties of dark bread and *knackebrod*, a hard biscuit flavored with dill or fennel seeds. Desserts often consist of cheeses, fruits, perhaps pudding or fresh-baked cakes.

In Germany, the last country in the watershed, Christmas likewise is strongly influenced by ancient pagan traditions overlaid with those from early Christian times. Particularly in Luther's day northern Germans thought of the 12 days from Christmas to Epiphany as demonic—possessed by the devil himself. In one of his table talks, Luther mentions "the presence of many devils in the forests, in the lakes, on the heaths as well as in the many damp dark cellars of northern Germany—devils that could harm people; devils also in the heavy clouds and dark overcast skies that produce hail, lightning, and thunder to poison the atmosphere."

In this dark northern European wintertime it is not surprising that lights, particularly candles, carry powerful symbolic meaning for all inhabitants. While scholars are not sure of the exact month in which Christ was born, they all agree that it could not be better positioned on the calendar than at the winter solstice, the darkest day on earth. How better to convey the true meaning of Christmas to a simple folk than this: the coming of light to redeem humankind from the darkness.

Advent in Germany is celebrated with stern intent. Wreaths with four candles can be found in homes, in churches, and often in public places and offices. One candle is lighted the first week of Advent, two the second week, and so on, until four candles are burning the final week before Christmas. What a beautiful crescendo of light even as the earth plunges ever more deeply into its annual darkness! Most German homes also have an Advent calendar with windows that the children open with each passing day of anticipation. Less frequently, but perhaps more symbolically, in some sections of Germany families display an Advent house with stained-glass windows behind which are small candles that are lighted when the windows are opened.

Unknown in the Scandinavian countries to the north but quite common in Germany is the figure of St. Nicholas who delivers presents to good children on December 6. He is not without his demonic side, for in most areas he is accompanied by his mentor, Ruprecht, who is dressed in black. While St. Nicholas usually appears in the form of a bishop carrying his crozier, Ruprecht sometimes is referred to as "Black Nicholas." His duty is to admonish children and, if necessary, administer a few swats to those who have misbehaved.

*T*he Feast of St. Lucia is commonly celebrated on December 13, though somewhat less exuberantly in northern Germany than in Sweden. Instead of the youngest daughter serving family members coffee and cakes in bed, the school children of the community join together in the evening for a *lichterzug*, a lantern procession through downtown. Often the lanterns are made by school children in their crafts classes out of wooden or wire skeletons covered with stretched material, painted colorfully, and housing a lighted candle. Sometimes the lanterns take the form of dollhouses in which the lighted candles silhouette the windows for the approving crowds lining the streets.

Now waning is the old Germanic tradition of whole communities gathering on a hilltop on December 21 for a festival of light. According to former practice, peasants prepared a huge wheel by stuffing straw between the spokes. During this, the darkest night of the year, everyone gathered to see the wheel, its straw torched, bounding down the hill like a dying sun, spinning bits of flame in all directions until it came to rest and to extinction in the dark valley below. December 21 is also the feast of St. Thomas, one of the 12 disciples. It occurs during the so-called time of raw nights and is overlaid with many superstitious customs. In a few communities, children simply receive special cookies on December 21. In others, certain signs in the sky are supposed to predict the future. In still others, children are threatened that they must be good or be punished by the so-called *Thomasnigl* (Thomas Nicholas), obviously a mistaken identification with the figure of Ruprecht mentioned above. All of this ties in linguistically with ancient custom, for indeed the German word for Christmas, *Weihnachten,* comes from the ancient plural form meaning "during the holy nights," the time when the gods of good and evil wander the earth before returning to Valhalla.

*T*he origin of the Christmas tree has been popularly ascribed to Martin Luther. It adapts the pagan use of the evergreen to symbolize everlasting life. The tree is scrupulously lighted in the German home only with candles, thus superimposing on the natural symbol of perpetual life one that connotes the supernatural. The move from the pre-Christian evergreen of the solstice to the lighted Christmas tree is but a small leap. Christ, the light of the world, was never more aptly depicted.

On Christmas Eve, if possible to the melody of *Stille Nacht, Heilige Nacht,* children gain their first glimpse of the lighted Christmas tree, which illuminates the many gifts strewn below. These were not brought by Santa Claus or any carry-over from St. Nicholas, nor even through the efforts of a good elf as in the Scandinavian countries, but by the *gabenbringer* (literally gift bringer) whom everyone recognizes to be the Christ child. Sometimes attributed to the *Weihnachtsmann* (Christmas man) or an angel, the gifts are prepared and kept in a locked room. The children are not permitted to enter the room before Christmas Eve when the doors swing open and the scene erupts in all its lighted glory. Most family members gather around the tree holding hands while they sing several hymns or carols before *bescherung,* the distribution of gifts.

A three-day event in Germany, Christmas lasts from December 24-26. The first two days are essentially for the family, the third for visiting relatives. Although southern Germans celebrate a number of feast days between Christmas and Easter, the somewhat more subdued northern Germans explode exuberantly on Sylvester (New Year's Eve). Firecrackers and shotguns thunder forth to bring good luck as well as to frighten off witches. The German Christmas finally twinkles out with Epiphany but not without another burst of lights. This time the *sternsinger* (groups of caroling children) roam the streets carrying star-shaped lanterns to symbolize the Wise Men from the East. Usually such children wear long white gowns, some even have kingly crowns on their heads.

When they have finished their rounds, in many German homes families gather one last time around the Christmas tree. They sing a few songs, enjoy the loot from neighborhood visits, and for the last time that season extinguish the candles burning brightly on the tree. The Christmas season, the feast of lights during the dark days of winter, has officially ended.

Born for a Cross

STANLEY L. STIVER JR.

Over 1900 years have passed since a simple wooden cross was erected at Calvary. Today the cross is the one universally recognized symbol of Christianity.

However, in the first three centuries after the death and resurrection of Jesus, the cross was not openly used as a Christian symbol. This was due, in part, to the persecution suffered by the earliest believers. Christians in Rome held secret worship services in the catacombs beneath the city, using a religious symbol whose significance could be hidden. One such symbol, the anchor cross, has been found in the ancient section of the Roman catacombs Callixtus and Domitilla. The anchor, a sign for fishermen, contained a crossbar and so was adopted as a disguised cross. The anchor itself was also a symbol of hope, perhaps stemming from these words to the Hebrews: "We have this as a sure and steadfast anchor of the soul, a hope" (Hebrews 6:19). As such, the anchor has been called both "the cross of the catacombs" and "the cross that is not a cross."

Another disguised cross was the tau cross, formed as the Greek letter T. This mark was used by the Hebrews when they wrote with blood on their doorposts on that first Passover in Egypt. It was also said to have been the shape of the standard on which Moses raised the bronze serpent in the wilderness. The tau cross with its several meanings has been called "the cross of many names."

A variation of the tau cross was the ankh, a cross with a loop at the top. The ankh was the Egyptian hieroglyphic for "life" and can be seen on ancient obelisks in Istanbul and Turkey, on the Hippodrome, and on the golden mask of King Tut. It was adopted by the Coptic Church of Egypt because Christ is the "tree of life."

The Emperor Constantine's vision of the cross in 312, his official recognition of Christianity by the Edict of Milan in 313, and the discovery of the "true cross" in Jerusalem by Constantine's mother, Helena, in 326 began to stimulate public acceptance of the undisguised cross. At this time, Constantine also abolished punishment by crucifixion in honor and in memory of the passion of Christ. In the Roman forum Constantine erected a statue of himself holding a cross-shaped lance. The cross also appeared on the imperial diadem, scepter, and coinage. He replaced the Roman eagles and the thunderbolts on the Roman Empire banners with the cross.

When Christianity became the official religion of the empire, the cross that was seen in public and carved on monuments was the simple Latin cross. This cross is the most familiar. It has a long vertical arm and a shorter horizontal one higher up. This was the way the cross appeared in the fourth and fifth centuries.

About the sixth century artists, desiring to decorate or embellish the plain cross, pointed out that Jesus called himself "the Lamb of God." Therefore, a lamb was artistically placed on the cross. The Greek Fathers at the Council of Trullo, 692, felt that the time had come for a more emphatic assertion of the personality and human nature of the Redeemer in sacred art. They decreed: "Instead of a lamb, our Lord Jesus Christ should be shown hereafter in his human form."

The earliest crucifix probably had the figure of Christ etched on it. The Christ generally was shown dressed in a robe reaching to his feet; his outspread arms did not hang but lay straight across the transverse beam, and his feet were placed side by side upon a supporting ledge. The head was erect with a kingly crown, wreath, or diadem; the eyes were

Photo: Iona Cross

frequently open and looking forward. The side was not pierced and often the hands and feet showed neither wounds nor nail marks. With the Christ generally resting against the cross rather than being attached to it, it was a cross of the victorious Jesus reigning from the tree. In this early Christian period attention was focused more on the cross as a symbol of salvation than on the actual suffering of the crucified Christ.

Later, in the ninth and tenth centuries, Christ was painted on the cross with his eyes closed, his head falling to his right shoulder (perhaps in the direction of the good thief), and his feet parallel on a footrest. During the 11th and 12th centuries the robe he wore was shortened to the knees and gradually to the loincloth. Francis of Assisi is credited with bringing a suffering Christ to the cross. Francis said: "Let us have a flesh and blood Christ on the cross; let us have the real thing." In the 13th century, complete realism in

depicting Christ on the cross was reached. Christ was then portrayed hanging on the cross wearing a crown of thorns, his diaphragm contorted with pain, his body twisted, his hands bent back, his face in agony, and blood flowing from his wounds. The knees were always bent, indicating pain. At the begin-

ning of the 14th century there was a sudden change in the position of Jesus' feet. Instead of being parallel on the bar piece and secured with two nails, his feet were superimposed and held by one nail. It is believed this change was done for artistic motives to bring a more moving and devoted pose.

The Crusades brought about a widespread erection of crosses and use of cross forms throughout Europe. At the Council of Clermont, France, in 1095, Pope Urban II, the motivator of the First Crusade, said to the crusaders: "The cross of Christ is the symbol of your salvation. Wear it, a red and bloody cross on your breast and shoulders, as a token that his help will never fail you, as the pledge of a man which can never be recalled." Knights could not be identified by the armor they wore, so they became identified by the color and design of the cross on their tunics and shields. The colors were: England, white; France, red; the

No event in the history of the world has so captured the imaginations of artists and poets as the life of Christ. Particularly, the events surrounding the birth and death of Jesus have received the most attention. Skilled artists on every continent have set their brushes to the recreation of these moments.

Although it may seem that the agony of Jesus' death on the cross is far removed from the excitement of the Bethlehem story, the drama is the same. The message of the angel to Mary, the resounding proclamation to the shepherds, and the extraordinary sign among the constellations of the night sky all point to the cross. The child born in the Bethlehem manger was born to die on a

cross. While it is the birth of Christ and the celebrations of that birth that receive the greatest public attention, it is the cross that has become the universally recognized symbol of the salvation wrought by him who was born in a stable.

The event of Calvary lifted the birth story to unknown heights and sent it soaring over national borders, over rivers and oceans, to encircle the earth. None who gathered at the Bethlehem stable would have suspected that in God's plan of recovery this child would be "wounded for our transgressions . . . bruised for our iniquities." Only someone who had lived with the vision of Isaiah could have seen the print of nails in the baby's hands and a cross silhou-

Flemish people, green; Italy, blue; the Knights Templar, red and white.

As Christian soldiers marched forth into battle, they carried a shield bearing the heraldic cross of their leader. Many new cross forms were developed, often by combining two or more forms to create a more distinctive identification. Many beautiful and unusual cross designs resulted. Never before in Christian history and at no time since have

Photos: St. Brigid Cross
Irish High Cross

people given such attention to the symbol of the cross.

In the 15th and 16th centuries, European adventurers took the cross with them as they explored the new land of America. On his first voyage, Christopher Columbus carried both the Spanish standard and a banner bearing a cross. A painting in the United States Capitol shows Columbus standing with a raised cross and an unfurled banner, taking possession of the land for God and for King.

The 17th century saw the rise of baroque art, with its use of dazzling materials. To the average person in those days this splendor compensated for the harshness of their everyday life. People were given palaces in the form of churches. The church building was the image of heaven on earth. Baroque artists continuously searched for the most dramatic moment. Christ was represented on the cross usually as a suffering Christ, with his head cast back, eyes lifted upward, mouth open in pain.

etted against the star-lit sky. Old Simeon caught a glimpse of the cross as he cradled the baby in his arms and said to Mary, "A sword will pierce your own soul also."

God had promised to send one who would restore the relationship between himself and his people. This one came as a child. The word became flesh. God became incarnate for the purpose of dying on the cross and rising again for our salvation.

The words, "O little town of Bethlehem . . . the hopes and fears of all the years are met in thee tonight," have meaning only because we also sing, "In the cross of Christ I glory, towering o'er the wrecks of time. All the light of sacred story gathers round its head sublime."

Crosses on gables and spires began to be popular, as evidenced by St. Peter's in Rome and St. Paul's in London.

Centuries ago it was the custom to erect stone or marble crosses in the marketplace to remind those who bought and sold to deal in a Christian manner.

Many legends have sprung up concerning the cross. In one elaborate tale, a branch of the tree of the

knowledge of good and evil is said to have been planted in Adam's grave. Later, Solomon had it cut down to use in building the temple, but it was found unsuitable. Instead it was used as a bridge across a brook. Later it was buried in the pool of Bethesda. At the time of the crucifixion it floated up and was used for Jesus' cross. After Jesus' death, his cross and those of the two thieves were buried. When the mother of Constantine went to the holy land seeking the cross of Jesus, she found that a temple had been built where the three crosses had been buried. The temple was pulled down, and in the digging the three crosses were found. However, they could not distinguish the true from the others. So, the body of a young man who had died that day was brought to the crosses, and each cross was in turn laid upon his body. When the true cross touched him, he came alive again. It still retained the power from the tree.

There are about 400 various cross forms, with perhaps 50 being the most familiar. These crosses consist of five basic forms. They are:

The tau cross. This T-shaped cross form is also called the pre-Christian or anticipatory cross because, with the loop added to the top to form a handle, it is identical with the Egyptian ankh or key of life.

The Latin cross. This common cross form is distinguished by an upright arm that is longer than the transverse arm. There are many variations of the Latin cross.

The Greek cross. This square, equal-limbed cross looks very much like the plus sign. Beauty-loving Greek artists recoiled from the cruelty suggested by the literal Latin cross and preferred to indicate the sacrifice by a square cross decorated with conventional designs rather than by an agonizing crucified figure.

The Eastern or Slavic cross. Greek Orthodox and Russian Orthodox churches both use the upright bar crossed by three transverse bars, of which the top transverse is shorter than the main transverse. The lower

Photos: Jerusalem Cross
Cross Botonée

crossbar or footrest, called the suppedaneum, is slanted.

The crosses of heraldry. Some of the cross designs that resulted from heraldry are St. Andrew's cross, the crosslet, the barbee and fitchee crosses. St. Andrew's cross is shaped like an *X*; the barbee is the fishers of men cross, with each end terminating in barbed fish hooks or fish spears; fitchee or the pilgrim cross is sharpened to a point at the bottom so that it might easily be driven into the ground as the pilgrim rested at night on his long journey to the holy land.

Of these fundamental types there are many variations.

St. Brigid Cross

In Ireland, St. Brigid is revered only less than St. Patrick. Brigid's emblem is a cross woven of rushes. In many districts people still weave these crosses on the eve of her feast day, February 1. They hang them inside the eaves of their homes or from the ceiling of the kitchen to invoke St. Brigid's blessing on the house and the land. The genesis of the emblem and the custom focuses on a pagan chieftain who lived in the neighborhood of Kildare. The man was dying, so some Christians in his household sent for Brigid to talk to him about Christ. When she arrived the chieftain was raving. As it was impossible to instruct this delirious man, hopes for his conversion were diminishing. Brigid sat down at his bedside and began consoling him. As was customary, the dirt floor was strewn with rushes both for warmth and cleanliness. Brigid reflectively stooped down and started to weave them into a cross, fastening the points together. The sick man asked what she was doing. She began to explain the cross, and as she talked his delirium quieted and he questioned her with growing interest. He believed and was baptized at the point of death. For this reason the primitive cross of rushes has been venerated in Ireland for 1500 years.

Irish High Cross

High crosses in Ireland were erected not to commemorate the

Photos: Russian Orthodox Cross
Penal Crucifixes

dead but to celebrate the everlasting victory of Christ's resurrection. Carved out of hard sandstone, their average height is 12 to 15 feet, with some as high as 21 feet. A circle intersecting the arms of the high cross signifies eternity. The circle is the Celtic cosmic symbol for the revolving sun, denoting resurrection, perfection, and timelessness. Sometimes the stone ring has been a sort of solid wheel. On many of these high crosses are carved spirals and interlacing designs. The carvings also include Bible stories, which are called sermons in stone. People who could not read could be told the story carved on the high cross.

The Irish Belleek replica of a 10th century high cross pictured is composed of three basic parts: the base, the cross, and the cap. The cap is shaped like a house with shingled roof and gabled ends, exacting the form of a wooden church. The cross has a ring surrounding the upper middle of the cross. The ring in most crosses is open.

Iona Cross

The Iona Cross, sometimes called St. Martin's Celtic Cross, is found on the island of Iona, 50 miles west of Scotland. The 14-foot high cross has stood for a thousand years 200 yards from the Iona cathedral. The center illustration on one side of the cross shows the Virgin and Child surrounded by angels. A lion is portrayed on each crosspiece. Beneath is a portrayal of Daniel in the lions' den, while still lower is a figure giving the benediction. The boy David, playing his harp to Saul, with intertwining serpents and circular bosses completes the obverse side. (Bosses are small protuberances, most in groups of five, symbolizing the five wounds of Jesus.)

Iona is an island about three miles in length and a mile across. St. Columba, considered the greatest of the itinerant saints of Ireland, in the year 563 went with 12 disciples to Britain. Looking for an island where he could practice Christianity, he found Iona. Scotland and Iona were dominated by the king of the Picts. According to Scottish legend, two years after Columba arrived he made the sign of the cross over the Pict royal house. The door immediately opened. He again made the sign of the cross over the head of the king, and the king dropped his sword from a withered hand which remained withered until the king believed in God. His hand was then restored.

Jerusalem Cross

The Jerusalem Cross was the coat of arms of the first ruler of the Latin Kingdom of Jerusalem, Godfrey of Bouillon, victorious in the Crusade of 1099. Later the cross was used extensively by the Crusaders. The Jerusalem Cross is a Greek cross with four Greek crosslets between the arms. The five crosses have been said to represent the five wounds of Jesus—in his hands, feet, and side. Another interpretation of this symbol is that the four small crosses represent the wounds of Jesus in his hands and feet and the large central cross shows forth his death to the world. Yet another meaning given is that the four small crosses symbolize the four corners of the earth and the large one, the church in Jerusalem. Another explanation says the five crosses represent the five crusader countries of Great Britain, France, Germany, Italy, and Spain. Still another theory is that the crosses symbolize the Savior and the four evangelists.

Cross Botonée

Cross Botonée (or Budded Cross) is a cross of heraldric design from the time of the Crusades. When heraldry first became popular in England, the Angevin kings were rulers and French was the language of the court and nobility. Because of this many of the cross forms designed during this period were given French names.

The arms of the Cross Botonée end in a trefoil, representing the Trinity of Father, Son, and Holy Spirit. It is sometimes called the Budded Cross because of the moderate form of the trefoil ends.

The Cross Botonée pictured is a mosaic pectoral cross. At the trefoils on the top and the bottom are Christmas roses; at the trefoil to the left is a column like that to which Christ was tied when beaten 39 times across the back before his crucifixion; on the right is a ladder such as the one used to take the body of Christ down from the cross. In the center is the monogram Chi-Rho, formed of the

first two letters of the name of Christ in Greek.

Angel Cross

Southeastern Spain is known for its medieval Castle of the Holy Cross and for its church in Caravaca, which houses a famous crucifix. This crucifix is carried through the streets every May in recognition of its healing power.

The legend of this cross is that when the Moors captured prisoners, they tested them to determine if they were good at a particular trade. If they were, their lives were spared. Thus, if they captured a cobbler, they would ask him to make a pair of shoes and if the shoes were satisfactorily made, they would spare his life. One day they captured a priest and they asked him what he could do and what tools he needed. The priest said he needed a table, three linen cloths, two candles, and a crucifix, also a cup, bread, and wine. The Moors produced everything they had, but no crucifix. They were about to put the priest to death when from the heavens two angels descended holding a cross which they held over the table while the priest said mass. His life was saved.

This ancient cross has two wide transverse bars; the head and arms of Christ are on the topmost bar and his feet, just below the center transverse, are affixed by a single nail. Mary, his mother, is situated below his feet between two cherubs, one on each side of the cross, holding it up. Because the angels are holding up the cross, it is called the Angel Cross.

The cross is designed to hold sacred relics within its two parts. It is a brass reliquary of the type affixed to doorways of old Caravaca houses, whose occupants say, "When the two parts of the reliquary open of their own accord, a storm is brewing."

St. Damian Cross

One day in the early 1200s, tradition tells us, Francis of Assisi was passing by the church of St. Damian in Assisi, Italy, when he felt an overwhelming impulse to go in and pray. The old church had once been a holy place, but it had fallen into

---

Photos: Angel Cross
       Coventry Cross of Nails
       Italian Wooden Crucifix

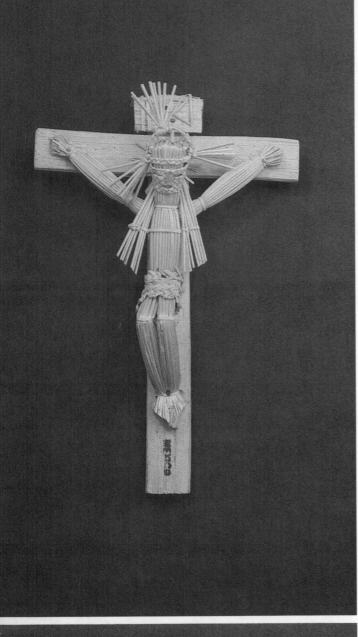

ruin. Inside the ruined walls of the church, where weeds were coming up through the paving stones, was a simple stone altar. A large painted wooden cross hung by a chain from the ceiling. Francis knelt before the altar and prayed for guidance. As he prayed, he looked at the large Byzantine crucifix. It represented Christ with head up and eyes looking out over the suffering world. The attitude of the figure was as though Christ was saying, "Come unto me." Francis gazed at the figure of Christ and proceeded to pray. Hearing a voice, he opened his eyes, looked about, and saw that he was alone. He believed he had heard the Lord speak to him and say, "Rebuild my church." He was sure that the voice came from the cross itself. He believed Christ had spoken to him. "Gladly, Lord," he said, "will I rebuild it." This Francis did.

This large wooden painted crucifix is still in existence today and can be seen at the Church of Santa Chiara at Assisi. There is a special chapel for this cross, and on the door entering into it are these words in several languages: "The cross that spoke to St. Francis."

Italian Wooden Crucifix

In Italy the transition from the triumphant Christ of the earlier centuries to the suffering Christ of the latter Middle Ages was made through the medium of cruciform panels. These painted wooden crosses had squared-off extremities. Economics influenced the development of this cross design, as wood was less costly than precious metals. There were three or four basic shapes of this cross, but many modifications of each. The crosses also varied in size—six, eight, ten, twelve feet long.

Sometimes called "inhabited crosses," the cruciform panels to the left and to the right of Christ were painted with images of his mother Mary and the beloved disciple John. They were also called "storied crosses" when there was not only a painted crucifix but also small scenes of the passion.

Cimabue (his real name was Cenni di Peppi) began painting the suffer-

Photos: Mexican Straw Cross
        Latin Cross with Skull and Crossbones

ing Christ in this style on the panels. He was the first to paint the body of Christ tautly S-shaped. The original of the cross pictured hung in the Franciscan church, Santa Croce (St. Cross) in Florence from the later 1200s until 1966, when it was destroyed in a terrible flood.

To prepare these wooden panels for painting they were first covered with a preparation of glue and plaster known as gesso. The paint was applied by the tempera method using powdered pigments mixed with egg and water. The backgrounds are usually burnished gold leaf. The results are strong, bright colors allowing the painting to be seen in the dim candlelit interiors of the churches.

Latin Cross
with Skull and Crossbones

The Latin cross is the most familiar form of the cross. Many times it is called the long cross because the cross has a long vertical arm and a shorter horizontal arm fairly high up. Its shape represents the cross of the crucifixion.

Often a skull and crossbones are shown just below the figure of Christ on this cross. The skull and crossbones represent Adam; their location at the foot of the cross is symbolical of the sin of humankind. The blood of the Lamb of God drips down upon it, washing away believers' sins.

Russian Orthodox Cross

The wooden, inlaid Russian Orthodox cross pictured here has two arms of equal length. The upper arm where the hands and the head of Christ would be, and the lower arm, the footrest, which is slanted at an angle less than 45 degrees from the horizontal bar. The origin of the slanting footrest is explained in various ways. The Russian Orthodox explain that Jesus was crucified with his feet side-by-side and not crossed over as is seen in many crosses. The footrest was supposedly wrenched from its normal position as Jesus, in his agony, pressed down on the footrest to get air into his lungs in his cramped suffering position. Others believe that after Jesus died, the Good Friday earthquake caused the footrest to slant. Many explain that the footrest is set at an angle to suggest St. Andrew's cross, as this apostle is believed to have introduced Christianity to Russia. St. Andrew, according to tradition, was put to death on a cross in the shape of an *X*. He is the patron saint of Russia.

This cross can be seen on the tombs of the czars and on the steeples over the onion-shaped domes of all three cathedrals in the Kremlin in Moscow.

German Wax Crucifix

Craftsmanship of a 500-year-old German folk art is seen in elegant wax castings drawn from antique wooden cookie molds. Clever or beautifully shaped cookies were a familiar part of nearly every Northern European holiday. Traditionally made of gingerbread, the cookies were formed by pressing the firm dough into laboriously handcarved baking forms. Close-grained fruitwood was the material of choice because it could tolerate the rough treatment of a working kitchen tool and still lend itself to a delicate line and fine detail.

The molds were highly prized as heirlooms and were handed down through the centuries from mother to daughter. Sold year-round at churches, shops, and country fairs, the cookies represented a lively and subtle form of communication—often using a traditional symbolic code to convey the message. They announced births and weddings, commemorated important holidays and deeply religious themes.

Nothing went to waste in those days. Because the dough was sweetened with honey, the bakers often used beeswax to cast the form. Ornamented with delicate colors, the beeswax castings became the forerunners of modern Christmas ornaments. Today, handpainted castings in a specially developed melt-resistant wax have been struck from the original forms.

The wax crucifix shown (c. 1800-1850) refers to Christ's passion. It might have been sold for a pilgrimage during the Easter season when spring thaws made traveling pleasant. The major use of such a cross, however, was to extend hospitality after a burial, a custom still practiced in Germany today. Since the message was one of joy, resurrection, and new life for the departed, the

facial expression is curiously cheerful for such a weighty theme.

Penal Crucifix

After the Irish Catholics were defeated by England and the Protestants at the Battle of Boyne in 1690, the Penal Laws were instituted. The Irish Parliament came under the control of the Protestants from 1692 until 1829. During this period of time Roman Catholic worship in Ireland was prohibited by law and Roman Catholic citizens were deprived of many of their natural rights of citizenship. A Roman Catholic was not permitted to hold office, serve as a juror, vote, attend public schools, or send children out of the country for schooling. They could not bear arms, could not be citizens of an incorporated town, could not own land. Anyone attending a Roman Catholic pilgrimage was subject to a fine and public whipping. No Roman Catholic prelate was allowed to reside in Ireland under the penalty of being hanged, drawn, and quartered.

The Penal Laws had the effect of making the Irish people more consciously and deliberately Roman Catholic than they had ever been before. The more savage the persecution, the more they clung to their faith. While the Penal Laws were in effect there were those who desired a symbol of their redemption. They made what has become known as the Penal Cross, a purely native carving. Most of the figures are of crude, unfinished workmanship. All the arms of the crosses are short, so the cross could be easily hidden in the sleeve. These penal crucifixes are uniquely Irish folk art objects. Each is carved from a single piece of wood and bears symbols of the passion. These are replicas of two of the Penal Crosses in the National Museum of Ireland in Dublin.

Mexican Straw Cross

Mexican Indians make these crosses from straw. Or, they may use palm leaves of various textures and thicknesses, twisting and plaiting them to make crosses. One of the unusual features of the straw cross is the mask on the face of Jesus. In

Photos: St. Damian Cross
Oberammergau Crucifix Carving

Mexico, masks are often placed upon statues and sculpture to animate them. The Mexican Indian believes masks are holy objects, having the power to confer upon the wearer the spirit of the diety portrayed.

Coventry Cross of Nails

On the night of November 14, 1940, the German Luftwaffe dropped fire bombs upon the industrial city of Coventry, England, the longest single night air raid upon any British city during the war. Fire bombs fell on the roof of the old cathedral, the church of St. Michael, built in the 14th century. The walls of the church were stone, as was the altar; but the roof and the ceiling were made of great oak beams. The bombs set the roof on fire. The next morning, all that remained were the stone walls and the stone altar. In the ashes people found many large forged medieval nails, four to five inches long, that had been used to secure the roof beams. Three of these nails were put together in the form of a cross. The Cross of Nails was taken to the stone altar and placed there. With chalk someone wrote on the front of the altar, "Father forgive."

This Coventry Cross of Nails has become a symbol of resurrection and reconciliation. It is a precious possession of the new Coventry Cathedral built after World War II. In the new cathedral, called the Coventry Cathedral of Resurrection through Sacrifice, the Cross of Nails is lodged at the heart of the altar cross, a glorious silver-gilt cross.

Ethiopian Coptic Cross

Ethiopia is one of the earliest Christian kingdoms in the world. Ethiopians apparently had contact with Christianity from the days of the apostles; the book of Acts tells of Philip explaining Isaiah to the eunuch who served Queen Candace of Ethiopia. A great king of the fourth century, Ezana, was converted to the Christian faith. The coins of his reign eventually had a cross on them, the first among the earliest coins of any country to carry the Christian symbol. In the 15th century Emperor Yaqob of Ethiopia decreed that every Christian should wear a cross.

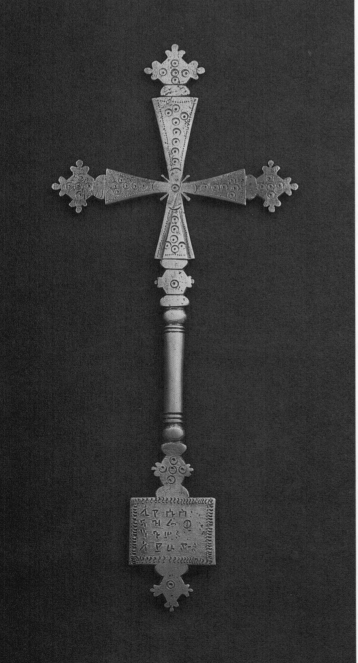

Photos: German Wax Crucifix
Ethiopian Coptic Cross

A week after a new birth, the Coptic priest is called by the baby's father to sprinkle the home with holy water. The priest will then arrange for baptism—for boys 40 days and for girls 80 days after birth. Baptism is a most complicated ceremony requiring the presence of several priests and deacons. A short neck cord called the *mateb* is tied around the neck of the child at Baptism, an indispensable part of the procedure. From this cord, a small cross will later be hung. The cross is the symbol that distinguishes an Ethiopian Christian from a Moslem or heathen. The small crosses worn by every Ethiopian Christian exist in an endless variety. There are 700 different designs found in Ethiopian crosses.

The cross pictured is the type carried by Coptic Orthodox priests. A blessing is given to the Christian by touching it to the forehead, the lips, and the breast. Larger crosses are used in processions and extra large ones are found on church doors. The cross inscription at the bottom of the cross is translated:

| Jesus | The Nazarene |
| King | Jews |

Oberammergau Crucifix Carving

In the 1200s when the monks in the monastery near Oberammergau saw that the soil in that region was not good for crops, they decided to teach the men of the town a different occupation—wood carving. The men became master carvers, passing the craft from father to son. Today there are 400 master carvers in Oberammergau, a town of 5000 residents. Most of the carving is from linden wood, a soft wood. The carving pictured, with a cross and figure of Christ, is of oak. An unusual feature of this carving is the top bar of the cross, which slants down on both sides. It is said that, because the weight of human sin on Christ became so heavy, the crossbar bent down at each end.

Planted in hate, the cross took root in believers' hearts as the emblem of Christian love. Brandished by Constantine, it emerged from the catacombs to crown cathedrals and emblazon crusader shields. As a visual expression of faith, the cross has soothed, comforted, and inspired millions of people.

Christmas Corners

With Lowly Folk

Excerpts from Luther's Christmas Story

ROLAND H. BAINTON

What Martin Luther has said about Christmas will affect the modern reader as diversely as the Christmas narrative itself. Some believe in the opening of the heavens, the song of the angels, and the incredible star. They may nevertheless miss the wonder of God made flesh, but at least for them there is no barrier of rejected legend. For others the Christmas story is a fair and unbelievable tale, hallowed by the aura of a vanished faith. To a degree any reader who enters into Luther at all will have to do so despite a rejection of some details. Even the most unquestioning person will scarcely take seriously his engaging fancy that God alternately turned the star on and off to encourage or discipline the Wise Men. But one can smile or chuckle at his debonair embellishments without rejecting the essential message of the man.

Luther's simplicity was due, of course, not to rationalism but to biblicism. He was not offended by miracle if it was in the sacred Word. But anything beyond the text of Scripture should be excised or at least subordinated. One might concede that Mary rode on a donkey from Nazareth to Bethlehem, but the gospel does not say so. The Wise Men might have been three, but the number was merely an inference from the three gifts.

For Luther the setting was his own section of Germany. Palestine was removed to Thuringia, and the distance from Nazareth to Bethlehem was as that from Saxony to Franconia. But it was in the field of emotion primarily that he invested the narrative with so deep a human quality. The distress of Mary, the misgiving of Joseph, the perplexity of the Wise Men, the cunning of Herod, all these are portrayed with the sort of human realism characteristic of historical novels, which develop biblical themes without ever caring whether they were in the first place literally so. Luther's interpretations of

Dr. Roland Bainton, distinguished Luther scholar, at a desk in Luther's study.

Christmas deserve reading, if for no other reason, because of the superb human delineations.

Luther did not believe lightly. He was simply amazed that all the characters in the Christmas story were themselves able to believe. Had he been in their places he would certainly not have done so. He was able to compose the incredulous reflections of Mary, Joseph, the shepherds, and the Wise Men because these were precisely the doubts with which he was wrestling.

Luther discerned that the greatest difficulty does not lie at the point of science, new or old. The question was not whether God could or would make a special star, but why the Lord of all the universe should care enough about us mortals to take our flesh and share our woes. The condescension of God was the great wonder. This it is that reason cannot fathom. Why should God humble himself to lie in the feedbox of a donkey and to hang upon a cross? The manger and the cross are never far apart for Luther. The birth was more than a lovely idyll. It took place in squalor and under the shadow of terror. Bethlehem presaged Calvary.

His conception of the nativity found expression in three forms: in sermon, in song, and in art. The most copious was preaching. Luther delivered between 150 and 200 sermons a year. He preached from two to four times on a Sunday and several times during the week at the university or in the household composed of children, servants, relatives, and student boarders. The Christmas theme might occupy him for more than a month out of the year, from the beginning of Advent on November 30 until Epiphany on January 6, the traditional date for the arrival of the three kings. In this article, extracts have been selected from the sermons ranging over 30 years' time and have been woven together into a consecutive narrative and commentary. The material has been reconstructed by way of condensation, transposition, and paraphrase.

Annunciation

Our Lord Jesus Christ was born of a line of ancestors whom the evangelist Matthew arranges with artistry into three groups of 14 patriarchs, 14 kings, and 14 princes. Among the latter were a number of disreputable characters, as we learn from the book of Kings. God holds before us this mirror of sinners that we may know that he is sent to sinners, and from sinners is willing to be born.

An angel was sent to make an amazing announcement to the Virgin Mary. We note that this angel was called Gabriel. The name means power. He was commander in chief of the heavenly host, the keeper of the sword, the marshal of the divine Majesty. A thousand angels were at his beck, and their radiance was more dazzling than a hundred suns. If angels should speak to us in the majesty they enjoy in the presence of God, we could not endure the sight. The name *angel* means "a messenger," and Gabriel, the chief, had already been used to carry a message to Zechariah.

The name of the maiden was Mary. The Hebrew form of the name is Miriam and means "bitter myrrh." Why she was given this name I do not know, save that the Jews had the custom of naming children from the circumstances of the birth. Now the time when Christ should come was one of utter bitterness and extreme poverty for the Jews. They were a downtrodden people and their lot was pitiable, like ours today so that all might well weep bitterly.

Among the downtrodden people she was one of the lowliest, not a maid of high station in the capital city, but a daughter of a plain man in a small town. We may infer that she was of no account because she herself said in her song, "He has regarded the lowly state of his maidservant." Who knows whether Joachim and Anna, her parents, were alive at the time? In all likelihood she was an orphan; nor is there the slightest ground for the legend that her parents were wealthy and divided the legacy into three portions, one for the Church, one for the poor, and one for Mary. In the village of Nazareth she appeared as a mere servant, tending the cattle and the house, and no more esteemed than a maid among us who does her appointed chores. Her age was probably between 13 and 15 years.

*A*nd yet this was the one whom God chose. He might have gone to Jerusalem and picked out Caiaphas' daughter, who was fair, rich, clad in gold-embroidered raiment, and attended by a retinue of maids-in-waiting. But God preferred a lowly maid from a mean town.

Quite possibly Mary was doing the housework when the angel Gabriel came to her. Angels prefer to come to people as they are fulfilling their calling and discharging their office.

"Dear Mary," said the angel, "the Lord is with you. Blessed are you among women." We are unable to tell whether Mary perceived at once that it was an angel who spoke to her. Luke seems to imply that she did not, because he indicates that she was abashed, not so much by his appearance, as by his words. And they were most unusual: "O Mary, you are blessed. You have a gracious God. No woman has ever lived on earth to whom God has shown such grace. You are the crown among them all." These words so overwhelmed the poor child that she did not know where she was. Then the angel comforted her and said: "Do not be afraid, Mary, for you have found favor with God. And behold, you shall conceive in your womb and bring forth a son, and shall call his name Jesus. He will be great, and will be called the Son of the Highest."

St. Bernard declared there are here three miracles: that God and man should be joined in this Child; that a mother should remain a virgin; that Mary should have such faith as to believe that this mystery would be accomplished in her. The last is not the least of the three.

Visitation

The angel Gabriel, after informing Mary that she was herself to become a mother while yet a virgin, conveyed the almost equally unbelievable news that her kinswoman Elizabeth had conceived in her old age and was already in her sixth month. Mary then arose "and went with haste into the hill country, to a city of Judah, and she entered the house of Zechariah, and greeted Elizabeth."

We observe that she went by the hill country, not by the plain. The journey would take her all of three days. We do not know the precise destination, for although Zechariah was a priest, he was not under the necessity of residing in Jerusalem. He was a poor priest, and we are not to think of Elizabeth as in a much more exalted station than Mary.

The evangelist Luke advisedly inserted those words "with haste." He meant that she did not stop every five paces to strike up a conversation. Mary was like a maid who sees and hears nothing save the commands of her mistress, or like a housewife who does not loiter here and there to chat. The mother of our Lord was no gossip. She went with haste.

"And it came to pass, when Elizabeth heard the greeting of Mary, that the babe leaped in her womb; and Elizabeth was filled with the Holy Spirit. And she spoke out with a loud voice and said, Blessed are you among women." Then Mary broke forth into singing. Her song is called the *Magnificat* because it begins with the words: "My soul magnifies the Lord, and my spirit has rejoiced in God my Savior. For he has regarded the lowly state of his maidservant."

They do Mary wrong who say that she gloried not in her virginity but in her humility. She gloried neither in her virginity nor in her humility, but solely in God's gracious regard. The stress should not be on the "lowly state," but on the word "regarded." Her lowly state is not to be praised, but God's regard, as when a prince gives his hand to a beggar, the meanness of the beggar is not to be praised, but the graciousness and goodness of the prince. The evil eye looks only on the reward and the result of humility. The genuinely humble look not at the outcome of their humility. True humility does not know that it is humble. If it did, it would be proud from the contemplation of so fine a virtue.

Mary's song continued: "For behold, from now on all generations will call me blessed. For he who is mighty has done great things for me; and holy is his name. And his mercy is on those who fear him from generation to generation. He has shown strength with his arm; he has scattered the proud in the imagination of their hearts. He has put down the mighty from their thrones, and exalted the lowly."

God allows the godly to be powerless and oppressed so that everyone thinks they are done for, yet even in that very moment God is most powerfully present, though hidden and concealed. When the power of man

The Visitation

fails, the power of God begins, provided faith is present and expectant. When the oppression is ended, then one sees what strength lies below the weakness. Even so was Christ powerless on the cross, and yet he was most mighty there and overcame sin, death, world, hell, devil, and all ill.

Mary's song went on: "He has filled the hungry with good things; and the rich he has sent away empty. He has helped his servant Israel, in remembrance of his mercy; as he spoke to our fathers, to Abraham, and to his seed forever."

You have got to feel the pinch of hunger in the midst of scarcity and experience what hunger and scarcity are, when you do not know where to turn, to yourself, or to anyone else but only to God, that the work may be God's alone and of none other. You must not only think

and speak lowliness, but come into it, sink in it, utterly helpless, that God alone may save you. Or at any rate, should it not happen, you should at least desire it and not shrink. For this reason we are Christians and have the Gospel, that we may fall into distress and lowliness and that God thereby may have his work in us.

Mary stayed with Elizabeth about three months, and then returned to her own house.

See how purely she leaves all to God, and claims for herself no works, honor, or reputation. She behaves just as she did before any of this was hers—seeks no greater honor, is not puffed up, vaunts not herself, calls out to no one that she is the mother of God, but goes into the house and acts just as before—milks cows, cooks, scrubs the kettles, and sweeps the house like any housemaid or housemother in the most menial tasks, as if none of these overwhelming gifts and graces were hers. Among the other women and neighbors she was esteemed no more highly than before and did not ask to be. She was still a poor townswoman among the lowliest. What a simple pure heart was hers! What an amazing person she was! What mightiness was hidden below her lowliness! How many there were who met her, talked with her, ate and drank with her, and perhaps looked down upon her, who, had they known, would have been overpowered in her presence.

Mary was engaged to marry a man named Joseph and "before they came together, she was found with child of the Holy Spirit." The Scripture says that "Joseph her husband, being a just man, and not wanting to make her a public example, was minded to put her away secretly."

We can see from this that Mary was a poor little orphan, without father and mother, about 14 years old. Joseph took pity on her and was betrothed to her lest she be deserted. If she had had parents alive, she would have been with them rather than with a husband. She was a bride, but had not gone to live with her husband and still wore the garb of a virgin. Joseph intended to take her to wife, and was very much disturbed when he discovered that she was with child. She had spent the previous three months with Elizabeth. Joseph could hardly place a good construction upon her condition. If the like had happened to you or me, what should we have thought? Had Joseph wished to follow the letter of the law, he would have denounced her and she would have been stoned. This was a grievous cross to Mary that her bridegroom should suspect and cast her off. The evangelist commends him for resolving to do it secretly. He thought to himself, "She is a poor girl and if I expose her she will go from bad to worse." He did not wish to have any court proceedings which would be damaging to her, although he considered her hopeless. This holy virgin, celebrated by all the prophets, was judged by her own husband to be a loose woman. But God inclines his ear to all who call upon him. An angel came from heaven and said: "Fear not. There is no dishonor or disgrace. She is with child by the Holy Spirit." Joseph had nothing to go by save the word of God, and he accepted it. A godless man would have said it was just a dream, but Joseph believed the word of God and took unto him his wife. Joseph kept the secret and none knew what the Holy Spirit was doing.

Nativity

The birth of Christ took place exactly when the emperor Augustus sent out a decree that all the world should be taxed. This was no accident. The birth of Christ was timed to coincide with the census because God wanted to teach us the duty of obedience even to a heathen government. Had he been born prior to the census, it might have appeared that he was unwilling to be subject to the Roman Empire. At the very first moment of his life, Christ and his parents had to give evidence of obedience, not to God, but to the heathen emperor, the enemy of the Jews. This is the strongest proof that Christ's kingdom is to be distinguished from that of the world. Christ did not wish to erect a kingdom like an earthly king, but wished to be subject to a heathen government.

The law of the census required that each householder must be present in his hometown at the time of the enrollment. Joseph was of the lineage of David and had to go to Bethlehem, the city of David. Despite his royal ancestry, he was so poor that he had been unable to make a living in Judah and for that reason had transferred to Nazareth. Now he had to go back. Scripture says that he took with him "Mary, his betrothed wife, who was with child." She would have had good reason to excuse herself from making the journey so close to her time, but she said nothing because she wished to trouble no one. They simply left the house. Perhaps they had a donkey for Mary to ride upon, though the Gospels say nothing about it and we may well believe that she went on foot.

The journey was certainly more than a day from Nazareth in Galilee to Bethlehem, which lies on the farther side of Jerusalem. Joseph had thought, "When we get to Bethlehem, we shall be among relatives and can borrow everything." A fine idea that was!

Bad enough that a young bride married only a year could not have had her baby at Nazareth in her own house instead of making all that journey of three days when heavy with child! How much worse that when she arrived there was no room for her! The inn was full. She had to go to a cow stall and there bring forth the Maker of all creatures because nobody would give way.

The birth was still more pitiable. No one regarded this young wife bringing forth her firstborn. No one took her condition to heart. No one noticed that in a strange place she had not the very least thing needful in childbirth. There she was without preparation: no light, no fire, in the dead of night, in thick darkness. No one came to give the customary assistance. The guests swarming in the inn were carousing, and no one attended to this woman.

Joseph had to do his best, and it may well be that he asked some maid to fetch water or something else, but we do not read that anyone came to help. Shame on you, wretched Bethlehem! The inn ought to have been burned with brimstone, for even though Mary had been a beggar maid or unwed, anybody at such a time should have been glad to give her a hand.

There are many of you in this congregation who think to yourselves: "If only I had been there! How quick I would have been to help the baby! I would have washed his linen. How happy I would have been to go with the shepherds to see the Lord lying in the manger!" Yes, you would! You say that because you know how great Christ is, but if you had been there at that time you would have done no better than the people of Bethlehem. Childish and silly thoughts are these! Why don't you do it now? You have Christ in your neighbor. You ought to serve him.

If Joseph and Mary had realized that her time was so close she might perhaps have been left in Nazareth. And now think what she could use for swaddling clothes—some garment she could spare, perhaps her veil—certainly not Joseph's breeches which are now on exhibition at Aachen.

The Adoration of the Shepherds

She "wrapped him in swaddling clothes, and laid him in a manger." Why not in a cradle, on a bench, or on the ground? Because they had no cradle, bench, table, board, or anything whatever except the manger of the oxen. That was the first throne of this King. There in a stable, without man or maid, lay the Creator of the world. And there was the maid of 15 years bringing forth her firstborn without water, fire, light, or pan, a sight for tears!

Think, women, there was no one there to bathe the baby. No warm water, nor even cold. No fire, no light. The mother was herself midwife and the maid. The cold manger was the bed and the bathtub. Who showed the poor girl what to do? She had never had a baby before. I am amazed that the little one did not freeze. Mary's eyes were moist even though she was happy, and aware that the baby was God's Son and the Savior of the world.

Shepherds

"And there were in the same country shepherds living out in the fields, keeping watch over their flock by night." That was a mean job, watching flocks by night. Common sense calls it low-down work, and the men who do it are regarded as trash. But the evangelist lauds the angels because they proclaimed their message only to shepherds watching their flock by night. These were real sheepherders. They stayed in their station and did the work of their calling. They were pure in heart and content with their work, not aspiring to be townsmen or nobles, nor envious of the mighty. Next to faith this is the highest art—to be content with the calling in which God has placed you. I have not learned it yet.

Look at the shepherds. They were watching their flocks by night, and an angel came and made them apostles, prophets, and children of God. Caiaphas, Herod, and the high priests were not deemed worthy.

The field was flooded with light—brilliant, dazzling. Not the town, but the field was lighted up. Why did not the angel go to Jerusalem? There was the worship established by God. There were the princes of the people and the rulers in church and state. There were the temple and the high priests ordained of God. Why did not the angel go to them? He went to Bethlehem, a dung heap compared to Jerusalem. And he did not go to the town of Bethlehem but to the shepherds.

Do not be afraid," said the angel. I fear death, the judgment of God, the world, hunger, and the like. The angel announces a Savior who will free us from fear. Not a word is said about our merits and works, but only of the gift we are to receive. "For there is born to you this day," that is, *to us*. For our sakes he has taken flesh and blood from a woman, that his birth might become our birth. I too may boast that I am a son of Mary. This is the way to observe this feast—that Christ be formed in us. It is not enough that we should hear his story if the heart be closed. I must listen, not to a history, but to a gift. If you hear that this child is yours, that takes root, and a man becomes suddenly so strong that to him death and life are the same.

"And suddenly there was with the angel a multitude of the heavenly host."

An innumerable multitude! There are more angels in heaven than blades of grass in all the gardens in the whole world. So many men have never lived on earth as there are angels in heaven. You would think that some of these angels might have gone to the baby Jesus to take him a golden cradle or a feather bed or some warm water. And why didn't they? They were singing that he is the Lord and Savior.

The joy was so great that the angels could not stay in heaven, but had to break out and tell man on earth. The angels proclaimed to the shepherds "tidings of great joy." This is a mighty comfort to us. What the world despised the angels honored. They would have had a much bigger celebration if God had allowed them, but he wished to teach us through his Son to despise the pomp of the world.

All the angels in heaven, not one excepted, sang, "Glory to God in the highest." They were filled with too great joy for words.

The angels sang that he should be the Savior of the whole world to free his people and save them from their sins. That he has done and still is doing. He is not the sort of Lord who fights with the sword and has to do with civil government. Rather he rules with the gracious preaching of peace. For that reason he is called Jesus, meaning a Savior who helps his people to turn and be saved.

This is a great miracle that the shepherds should have believed this message. They might easily have thought to themselves, "Are we two shepherds worthy that the whole host of heaven should be marshaled for us and all the kings on earth and the dwellers in Jerusalem should be passed by?" I know I would have appealed to common sense and I would have said: "Who am I compared to God and angels and kings? It is an apparition." But the Holy Spirit, who preached through the angels, caused the shepherds to believe.

"And . . . [the shepherds] came with haste and found Mary and Joseph, and the babe lying in a manger."

God is amazing. The babe is in a manger, not worthy of a cradle or a diaper, and yet he is called Savior and Lord. The angels sing about him, and the shepherds hear and come and honor him whom no maid serves as he lies with an ox and an ass. If I had come to Bethlehem and seen it, I would have said: "This does not make sense. Can this be the Messiah? This is sheer nonsense." I would not have let myself be found inside the stable.

Here we see that the preaching and singing of the angel were not in vain. However much the shepherds loved their sheep, they went at once to see the babe, whom the angels called the Lord. "And all they that heard it wondered at those things which were told them by the shepherds." Yes, but they did not remember them very long. For a quarter of a year anyone could have told how the child had been born at Bethlehem, how the angels sang and the Wise Men came from the East. But two, three, or four years afterward everyone had forgotten.

But Mary kept all these things in her heart, meditated upon them, and thought to herself: "This is wonderful news that I am the mother of the child whom the angels call Lord." Even though she was the mother and had borne the child, she had need to ponder these words in her heart, in order to strengthen her faith and increase her assurance. She reflected how these words corresponded to those of the angel: "He will be great, and will be called the Son of the Highest." The message of the angels fitted in exactly with the annunciation by Gabriel. This was to her a great joy and confirmation.

Herod

When the Wise Men received the divine revelation that the king of the Jews was born, they made straight for Jerusalem, for, of course, they expected to find him at the capital in a lordly castle and a golden chamber. Where else would common sense expect to find a king? But because they were so sure of themselves, the star left them. Then they were sorely tried, and had they relied solely on human wisdom, would surely have said: "Confound it! We have come all this way for nothing. The star has deceived us. The devil has led us by an apparition. If a king had been born, would he not be in the capital and in a palace? But when we come, the star disappears and we find no one who knows anything about him."

But having come, they decided to inquire of the king before returning. At their report, Herod the king "was troubled, and all Jerusalem with him." Why was Herod terrified and all Jerusalem with him? *He* had good reason to be afraid because he had tyrannized the Jews for 30 years. Though a foreigner, he was acquainted with the prophecy that the scepter should not depart from Jacob, and now that the time was fulfilled, he trembled and thought to himself: "I have been king for 30 years and now the people are getting ready to oust me and these foreigners come and ask openly in the city for the newborn king. That sounds bad."

Now Herod had a crafty plan. "The Jews," thought he, "will hide the truth from me, but I will find out the town where this king is to be born and also the time, and then if they hide him, I will catch him anyway. I will kill so many babies that he cannot escape." So he called the scribes to him and said, "Where is Christ to be born?" Then perhaps through fear, the scribes answered him that in the prophet Micah it is written that he should be born in Bethlehem.

Why did not the star take the Wise Men straight to Bethlehem without any necessity of consulting the Scriptures? Because God wanted to teach us that we should follow the Scriptures and not our own murky ideas.

Wise Men

Now the Wise Men had the faith to follow the word of the prophet Micah. They were not offended that the king was not born in Jerusalem. They left the temple and went to the cow stall.

If I had been there, I would have stayed in the temple and said: "God dwells here and if the child is to be found anywhere in the world, it will be where all the priests are gathered and God is served." We may profit from the example of these heathen, who took no offense when directed from Jerusalem, the great city, to little Bethlehem. They followed the Word, and God comforted them by putting back the star, which led them now to Bethlehem and to the very door where the young child lay.

You will notice that none of the Jerusalemites went along. They left the babe to lie where he was and did not go to him, though they might well have done so from the ends of the earth. But they let these foreigners go to find out where he was, while they neglected him through fear of the tyrant Herod.

"And when they had come into the house, they saw the young child with Mary his mother, and fell down and worshiped him."

Though they saw but a tumbled-down shack and a poor young mother with a poor little babe, not like a king at all, meaner than one of their own servants, they did not shrink, but in great, strong faith cast out all misgivings of common sense, and, following simply the word of the prophet and the witness of the star, they accepted him for a king, fell on their knees, worshiped him, and presented their treasures. The world would not have done so but according to her wont would have looked for a velvet cushion and a host of servants and maids. The world makes presents to those who already have enough, and, to provide them, snatches the bread from the mouths of the hungry who have nothing but what they earn with their bloody sweat.

Let us observe how these Wise Men took no offense at the mean estate of the babe and his parents, that we also may not be offended in the mean estate of our

The Adoration of the Magi

neighbor, but rather see Christ in him, since the kingdom of Christ is to be found among the lowly and the despised in persecution, misery, and the holy cross. Those who seek Christ anywhere else find him not. The Wise Men discovered him not at Herod's court, not with the high priests, not in the great city of Jerusalem, but in Bethlehem, in the stable, with lowly folk, with Mary and Joseph. In a word, they found him where one would have least expected.

"They presented gifts to him: gold, frankincense, and myrrh."

We can present our gifts in the same way as the Lord says: "Inasmuch as you have done it to one of the least of these my brethren, you have done it to me." He who gives of his goods to help the poor, to send children to school, to educate them in God's Word and other arts that we may have good ministers—he is giving to the baby Jesus.

Whatever Happened to Christmas?

A One-Act Play

PHYLLIS REYNOLDS NAYLOR

Characters
Old Mr. Marlow
Businessman
Woman with carriage
Three college girls
Two teenage brothers

Setting
A bench in a park. A few fir trees and a lamp post give the illusion of the outdoors. The lamp post is decorated for Christmas. Artificial snow on ground if possible.

Curtain rises.

Old Mr. Marlow sits alone on the bench, disgruntled, hands in the pockets of his overcoat. A businessman with a briefcase hurries by without speaking. Mr. Marlow glowers at him. A woman with a baby carriage passes from the opposite direction, absorbed in a shopping list in one hand. Mr. Marlow glowers at her also.

Mr. Marlow: Bah! Humbug! What kind of Christmas do they call this, anyway? Rush, rush, rush. Hurry, hurry, hurry. Nobody's even got the time of day for you anymore.

Three college girls come hurrying across the stage, stumbling over Mr. Marlow's outstretched feet. They apologize as he gruffly tucks his feet back under bench, then hurry on.

Mr. Marlow: They don't even know what Christmas is *supposed* to be like. Tradition. That's what's missing. Christmas is nothing but a ruddy race course. In my day, we'd get up on Christmas morning, take the sled, and go off in the woods looking for the yule log—biggest one we could find. We'd bring it home, singing at the top of our lungs. Why, a log like that would last us almost till New Year's.

Offstage comes the boisterous singing of "Deck the Halls." Mr. Marlow leans forward and looks in the direction of the singing. Two teenage boys come into view, pulling a sled loaded with large packages, wrapped in brown paper and decorated with Christmas seals, ready for mailing. As they pass the park bench, a couple packages fall off.

Mr. Marlow: Whoa, there! Wait a minute, fellas! You lost something!

The boys stop and come back to get the boxes.

First boy: Hey, thanks. I'd hate to get all the way to the post office and find out we'd lost half our load.

Mr. Marlow: Looks like you're supplying presents for half the state of Ohio.

First boy: (*smiling*) Big family. We're spread all over the country and never get together for Christmas, but we always send gifts.

Mr. Marlow: (checking the address on one of the boxes) Must cost a small fortune to mail these all the way to Oregon.

Second boy: (laughing) More than the present's worth, usually. But it's the meaning of it, you know? It just wouldn't be Christmas if we didn't send a box.

The boys disappear offstage, singing again. Mr. Marlow leans back, watching them go. He faces the audience.

Mr. Marlow: Humph. Not exactly the kind of Christmas I remember, but. . . . Well, a custom's a custom, I guess. In my day, you knew it was Christmas the minute Thanksgiving was over, because the smell of turkey was replaced with the fragrance of fruitcake and apple turnovers and all the butter cookies you could eat.

There is laughter offstage, and the three college girls come back carrying sacks of groceries. They stop and whisper among themselves, then approach Mr. Marlow.

First girl: Excuse me, but would you possibly know where we could buy some sesame seed oil?

Mr. Marlow: Come again?

First girl: Sesame seed oil. We need it to bake a special cake, and the health store's all sold out. Oh, I'm sorry. I figured that . . . well . . . you being . . . you being a senior citizen and everything, you must be into health foods and you just might know of another store around here.

Mr. Marlow: (suppressing a smile) Well, girlie, I must be doing something right because I'm going to be 79 next month. But I sure never drank any sesame seed oil.

Second girl: Hey! Congratulations! If we knew where you lived, we'd bake you a cake. I mean, 79. Wow!

Third girl: We always give this big Christmas party for our friends, see. Everything's natural—organic all the way. It's delicious!

Second girl: Sort of a tradition, you know? Listen, would you like to come? We could celebrate your birthday in advance.

Mr. Marlow: (staring in surprise) Well . . . I . . . uh. . . .

First girl: (getting out a pen and piece of paper) Here's our address and the date and time. Look. We'll *expect* you! You'll be the guest of honor. If you've never had a natural foods meal, you don't know what you're missing.

Third girl: You'll come, now?

Mr. Marlow: My curiosity's got the best of me.

First girl: Good! Merry Christmas!

Mr. Marlow stares after them as they exit, taking off his hat and scratching his head in bewilderment.

Mr. Marlow: What's happened to Christmas? I've just been invited to a party, and I don't even know their names! (turns and stares at audience) They don't even know *my* name! Is it proper? Is it legal? (begins to smile) By jove, I'll go!

The businessman returns, whistling, a sprig of holly in his lapel, and drops a dollar bill in Mr. Marlow's upturned hat.

Businessman: Merry Christmas.

Mr. Marlow stares at the dollar in his hat and then at the businessman who is exiting offstage.

Mr. Marlow: Wha . . .? (stares at the dollar again, then quickly puts hat back on, holding the dollar)

The woman with the baby carriage comes back from other direction, more slowly now, presents stacked on top of the baby, humming a carol.

Woman: (smiling at Mr. Marlow) Merry Christmas.

Mr. Marlow: And a Merry Christmas to you, ma'am. (leans forward and looks at baby beneath all the packages) Here's a dollar for the little tyke. Buy him a chocolate Santa.

Woman: Why . . . why, thank you! But he's only two months old!

Mr. Marlow: Buy him some chocolate milk, then.

Woman: That's very kind of you!

The woman exits. Mr. Marlow settles back with a smile on his face, shaking his head in amusement.

Mr. Marlow: In my day, you knew the names of everybody in town. You knew exactly who would be coming to your house for Christmas—the whole tribe, that's who. Everybody had a place to go. Everybody belonged somewhere. Relatives weren't scattered around the 50 states. (shakes head thoughtfully) It's different now.

There is more boisterous laughter offstage, and the two teenage boys enter once more with their empty sled on the way back from the post office.

First boy: (gliding in on sled standing up) Whee! I'm an airboat!

Second boy: Airboat, my foot! You almost broke your neck back there. If you ever try a belly flop, you'll bust your head. (They stop in front of Mr. Marlow.)

First boy: Sort of cold to be sitting out here on a park bench, isn't it? You live down our way? How about a ride?

Mr. Marlow: A ride?

Second boy: Sure. Give us the directions and we'll pull. We owe you a favor, anyway.

Mr. Marlow: Well, I . . . .

First boy: Come on. We'll take it slow.

With a funny, quizzical look at the audience, Mr. Marlow eases himself up from the park bench and slowly lowers himself down on the sled, grinning as he finally settles down. He talks aloud to himself.

Mr. Marlow: Boy, oh, boy, Christmas is different, all right. And maybe that's not so bad. (then talking to the boys) Okay, young fellas, straight down the hill, turn right at the bottom, and don't stop for love or money. Whoopeeeeee!

The boys charge forward. Mr. Marlow rears back momentarily, clutching the sides, and the sled takes off as the curtain closes.

Our Christmas

Christmas Eve _____
_____
_____
_____

Christmas Day _____
_____
_____
_____

Christmas Worship _____
_____
_____
_____

Christmas Guests   **Christmas Gifts**
_____   _____
_____   _____
_____   _____
_____   **Christmas**   _____
_____   **Photo**   _____
_____   _____
_____   _____
_____   _____